C6 LT

JOURNALI
GRIFFITH
South Ci
Tel. 4

GW00728824

AUSTRALIA

The Law Book Company
Brisbane • Sydney • Melbourne • Perth

CANADA

Carswell
Ottowa • Toronto • Calgary • Montreal • Vancouver

Agents

Steimatzky's Agency Ltd., Tel Aviv;
N.M. Tripathi (Private) Ltd., Bombay;
Eastern Law House (Private) Ltd., Calcutta;
M.P.P. House, Bangalore;
Universal Book Traders, Delhi;
Aditya Books, Delhi;
Macmillan Shuppan KK, Tokyo;
Pakistan Law House, Karachi, Lahore.

Journalists and the Law

YVONNE MURPHY

ROUND HALL SWEET & MAXWELL
DUBLIN

Published in 1997 by
Round Hall Sweet & Maxwell
Brehon House, 4 Upper Ormond Quay,
Dublin 7.

Typeset by
Gough Typesetting Services, Dublin.

Printed by
Colour Books, Dublin

ISBN 1-899738-36-3

A catalogue record for this book
is available from the British Library.

PREFACE

This book is designed principally for students of journalism, media studies and related areas. It is hoped that working journalists will also find it useful.

The book seeks to redress two main needs. The first is to give readers a sound general overview of the legal system, specifically the courts and the reporting thereof and the legal profession. There is an increasing public interest in the working of the courts and legal affairs in general. For most people, journalists are the principal source of information on these topics.

Secondly, the book addresses the areas of the law which are of most interest to journalists in their day to day work. The areas of libel, contempt and relations with sources are of significant interest to working journalists. I have tried to steer a middle course between the complexities of the technical works on the subject and the very brief handbooks which are often the only alternative. The treatment of the technical areas is perhaps fuller than usually found in books for a non-legal audience. It may in the end prove more digestible.

Particularly in relation to libel, an effort is made to go beyond the details of the law into their practical application in actual cases. There is a considerable emphasis on tactical as well as technical aspects. It is hoped that the chapter on pleadings and other procedural steps will enable practising journalists to feel less excluded from the process of preparation for trials than is often the case at the moment.

Yvonne Murphy

Dublin,
December 1996

CONTENTS

GLOSSARY OF LEGAL TERMS

ab initio: from the outset.

ascond: to hide from or otherwise to evade the jurisdiction of the court.

accessory, before the fact: one who, though absent at the time of commission of a felony, assists or commands another to commit the felony; **after the fact:** one who, though not present at the time of commission of the felony, actively assists a felon to avoid justice knowing that a felony has been committed.

accusatorial/adversarial system: a legal system where the responsibility to collect and present evidence lies with the party who seeks to introduce the evidence. In criminal matters the accused person is presumed to be innocent until proven guilty and the onus of proving guilt rests on the prosecution.

adverse possession: the acquiring by a squatter on property of rights of ownership to that property by flux of time.

aid and abet: to intentionally assist a person committing a crime.

affidavit: a written and sworn statement made by a person who is called a deponent.

affray: fighting by two or more persons in a public place which is of such a nature as would frighten reasonable people.

a fortiori: much more so and with greater force.

aggravated murder: murder of a member of the security forces or a member of a foreign government or diplomatic corps or murder committed in the course of certain offences as detailed in the Offences Against the State Act 1939.

aggravated sexual assault: a sexual assault involving serious violence or the threat of serious violence or the infliction of humiliation, degradation or a grave nature. Criminal Law (Rape) Amendment Act 1990.

alibi: a defence to a criminal charge to the effect that the accused was elsewhere when the crime was committed.

anton piller order: *see* **Injunction.**

apology and offer to make amends: a factor which a court can take into account in assessing (and reducing) damages payable by a defendant in defamation proceedings.

appearance: *see* **pleadings**.

appellant: a person who appeals.

apportionment of fault: a judge hearing a case where there is more than one defendant can hold both defendants liable to varying degrees expressed as percentages of the overall award made to the plaintiff. Also liability as between the plaintiff and defendants can be apportioned to reflect the plaintiff's own contributory negligence.

attachment and committal: the process whereby a person is brought before a court to explain their contempt of a court order (attachment) and their commital to prison for contempt upon failure or refusal to comply with the order of the court or to otherwise purge their contempt.

articles of association: *see* **Memorandum and Articles**.

arraignment: the commencement of a criminal trial when the charges against the accused are read out in court and the accused is asked whether he/she pleads guilty or not guilty.

audi alteram partem: (hear the other side) a rule that requires a court or tribunal to hear both sides of a matter before it. *See* **Fair procedures**.

auditor: an independent professional who undertakes to audit the books of account of a company and who must certify that the books are being properly kept.

bail: the process whereby a person accused of a criminal offence is set free until the date of the trial. An independent surety is required who is a person who undertakes to have the accused person in attendance at the trial. A bail bond is a sum of money usually provided by the surety which is lodged in court and is forfeitted if the accused does not turn up for the trial.

bailiff: a person employed by the sheriff to serve and execute writs and orders (*see* **execution**).

balance of convenience: *see* **injunction**.

Balance of probability: the burden of proof resting on the plaintiff in a civil action. Essentially the plaintiff must prove that his version of events is more likely than not.

Bar Council: the governing body of the barrister's profession responsible for the internal regulation of the profession and external relations between the bar and other persons or groups.

barring order: an order preventing one spouse (or cohabiting partner) from entering the family home where the safety or welfare of the other spouse or of the children so requires.

battery: an unlawful touching of a person (a crime as well as a tort).

bench warrant: an order of a court for the immediate arrest of a person frequently issued where a person fails to appear at trial in a criminal case.

beyond reasonable doubt: the burden of proof in a criminal case. If there is any reasonable doubt regarding the evidence against an accused person, he/she is entitled to the benefit of the doubt and must be acquitted.

bill: a piece of draft legislation.

binding to keep the peace: an order made by a criminal court whereby a person undertakes to keep the peace for a specified time and be of good behaviour.

bona fide: in good faith, honestly, innocently.

book of evidence: statements of evidence and a list of exhibits upon which the prosecution intends to rely in a trial by jury. It must be served on the accused before his trial.

bye-law: a law passed by a local authority or other body to whom statutory authority is granted. A bye-law will be limited in its application either in terms of the area or the persons it affects.

camera, in: the hearing of a case in court where the public have been excluded in the interests of justice. Examples are cases involving infants, rape. matrimonial cases and applications for the appointment of an examiner.

capital murder: *see* **aggravated murder.**

care order: an order issued by the District Court on the application of a health board, committing a child to the care of the health board where there is physical or sexual abuse or neglect or where the child's health, development or welfare is or is likely to be adversely affected.

case stated: a procedure for submitting a question or questions of law to a higher court to be determined. The points raised are argued before the higher court which makes a determination and then remits the matter back to the original court for disposal. A case may be stated on the application of either party or by the court of its own motion.

causation: the necessary link between a persons actions and the eventual consequences of those actions. There must be a sufficient link between the actions and consequences for liability to attach to a person in crime or in tort.

cause of action: the facts which give rise to proceedings in a court.

certiorari: where an inferior court or tribunal or person exercising a legal power makes an error or fails to apply fair procedures before reaching its decision an aggrieved party can apply to the High Court by way of Judicial Review for an order of Certiorari invalidating or quashing the decision (*see* **judicial review, natural justice, fair procedures**).

chancery: general description of cases involving the application of the law of equity to a particular dispute. Such cases are generally heard in the Chancery lists of the High Court and will typically involve injunctions and certain company law matters such as liquidations and receiverships.

charge: in the criminal law context an instruction to a jury issued by the trial judge which summarises the evidence and outlines the applicable law.

chattels: items of property which are not freehold real property. Generally a chattel will be an item of personal property.

Chief Justice: the president of the Supreme Court and the most senior judge in Ireland.

circumstantial evidence: evidence which indirectly points to a particular conclusion on an issue in a case but which does not directly prove the issue.

civil bill: a document which initiates civil proceedings in the Circuit Court and which sets out the factual basis of the claim and the nature of the relief sought by the plaintiff.

civil process: a document initiating a civil claim in the District Court setting out the facts and the nature of the relief sought by the plaintiff.

civil law: depending on the context civil law is the body of law providing a citizen with a civil remedy (such as damages) and is contrasted with criminal law which involves the imposition of a penal sanction (such as imprisonment) on an offender. Civil law can also be contrasted with canon law (the law of the Roman catholic church). In addition a system of law which relies on a written code rather than a body of judge made law is described as a civil law system. The Irish system is not based on such a code and thus in this context has what is called a common law system.

close of pleadings: the stage in civil litigation when all matters in issue between the parties have been set out in the pleadings (*see* **pleadings**).

codicil: an addition to or amendment of or explanation of a will but created after the execution of the original will.

commissioner for oaths: a person appointed to administer oaths to persons making sworn statements such as affidavits or statutory declarations.

common law: a system of laws not based on a written code but based on a body of laws derived from decisions of judges in previous cases. However written laws exist within a common law system and these laws are distinguished from common law by describing them as statute law.

company: a legal entity which has a legal personality separate and distinct from its members. It has separate rights and duties under the law and can sue and be sued in its own name. A limited company is one where the liability of the members to discharge the company's debts in the event of insolvency is limited to a certain amount. A limited company which does not offer its shares to the public is a private limited company whereas a company which offers shares to the public is called public limited company or plc. Every company must have a set of rules which are contained in its Memorandum and Articles of Association. Every limited company must have Directors, a Secretary and Auditors and must file Annual Returns (which are statements of the company's financial results) and other documents with the Companies Office.

competition law: an area of law principally administered by the competition authority which governs monopolies, mergers, restraint of trade and the fixing of pricing by commercial entities. The U.S. equivalent is known as Anti-Trust Law.

complainant: a person who makes a complaint which gives rise to legal proceedings, *e.g.* the victim in a rape case.

concurrent sentences: separate sentences for separate offences which a judge orders to be served at the same time.

consecutive sentences: separate sentences for separate offences which a judge orders the accused to serve one after the other.

conspiracy: the crime of conspiracy is committed when two or more persons agree to effect an unlawful purpose. The tort of conspiracy is committed where two or more persons act with

the intent to damage the business of another and whose actions
cause such damage. A trade union organising a strike in relation
to a trade dispute is immune from liability in conspiracy in
circumstances set out by the Industrial Relations Act 1990.

constructive dismissal: the treatment of an employee by his
employers such that the employee is entitled to deem himself
to be discussed by the employer.

consumer affairs, director of: an independent office holder appointed by a minister with responsibility for dealing with
complaints against businesses from members of the public and
given certain powers to take action against businesses in breach
of consumer protection legislation.

contempt of court: failure to comply with a court order or conduct
which is likely to prejudice the fair trial of an accused person
or other conduct which is disrespectful of the court. Contempt
is punishable by imprisonment.

contributory: a person who is liable to contribute to the assets of
a company in the event of its being wound up.

contributory negligence: a degree of fault on the part of the
plaintiff in an action for damages which reduces his damages
by an amount expressed as a percentage of the total award made
by the trial judge.

conveyancing: the legal work involved in purchasing or selling real
property.

counterclaim: a claim made by a defendant in an action which is
pursued in the same action against the plaintiff.

court of first instance: the court where any matter is first heard
and determined.

crime: an offence contrary to public law which gives rise to a penal
sanction.

cross appeal: where both parties appeal the decision of a court.

damages: a sum of money awarded to a person to compensate him
for his loss. General damages are those damages which cannot
be ascertained other than by a judicial assessment *e.g.* damages
for pain and suffering. Special damages are those amounts which
are capable of precise calculation in advance of the hearing, *e.g.*
medical expenses. Punitive or exemplary damages are awarded
to a plaintiff in exceptional circumstances not to compensate the
plaintiff but to punish the defendant. Nominal damages are

awarded where the plaintiff has succeeded but has sustained no loss and contemptuous damages are awarded where it is thought necessary to express contempt for the plaintiff's conduct by a very small award.

data protection: statutory protection of information concerning individuals which is stored electronically. Persons storing such information are under obligations imposed by the Data Protection Act 1988 regarding their use of such information. Responsibility for supervising compliance with the act rests with the Data Protection Commissioner.

de facto: a situation or state of affairs which exists in fact.

de jure: a situation or state of affairs which exists as a matter of law.

debenture: in company law, an instrument or deed whereby a company acknowledges its indebtedness to a particular person, which is issued as security for a loan advanced to the company.

declaration: an order of the High Court which declares the rights of a person in the particular circumstances before the court. Most commonly sought in Chancery and judicial review proceedings.

decree: an order of a court. A decree nisi is a conditional order and a decree absolute is a final decree.

deed: a legal document which is formally sealed.

declarent: a person making a statutory declaration.

defence: a document which sets out the nature of a defendant's intended defence to a civil action.

delegated legislation: written laws in the form of orders, bye-laws or statutory instruments made by a person or body under authority provided by an act of the Oireachtas.

deponent: a person making an affidavit.

discovery: any party to a civil action has the right, before the trial of the action, to view and copy documents which are in the possession of or can be obtained by the other party, which are relevant to the proceedings between the parties. Discovery can be made on a voluntary basis or pursuant to an order of the court but in either case an affidavit is required by the party discovering the documents.

disqualification order: company law; an order made by the High Court preventing a person from being an officer or servant or receiver or liquidator of any company.

embezzlement: a criminal offence committed by a person who fraudulently converts to his own use, property received by him on account of his employer.

Employment Appeals Tribunal (E.A.T.): an industrial tribunal set up by the Redundancy Payments Act 1967 and modified by the Unfair Dismissals Act 1977,whose purpose is to adjudicate on disputes relating to the termination of employment. The tribunal can award damages of up to two years remuneration or reinstatement (returning the employee to his former job with back pay and preserved benefits) or re-engagement (return to former job on terms fixed by the tribunal). There is a right of appeal to the Circuit Court from a decision of the Tribunal and a further right of appeal to the High Court.

equality officer: a person appointed by the Labour Relations Commission whose function is to investigate complaints by employees in relation to the Employment Equality Act 1977 or the Anti-Discrimination (Pay) Act 1974. Following an investigation and oral hearing the Equality Officer makes a recommendation which can be appealed by either side to the Labour Court.

Equity: a body of law which developed in the old courts of chancery parallel to the common law and originally addressed itself to the defects of the common law. Equity provided remedies such as injunctions and specific performance where the common law could only offer damages. Equity now co-exists with common law and equitable as well as common-law remedies can now be sought in the same court.

Used in a broader context equity can also mean simply the requirements of fairness and justice. In the context of company law equity share capital denotes the type of share where the shareholder is not guaranteed a fixed dividend but will receive a dividend commensurate with the company's financial results.

estoppel: a principle of equity whereby a person's behaviour prevents him from relying on a particular argument which but for his behaviour would otherwise have been available to him.

ex parte: an application which is made to a court without notice to the other party and where the other party has no right to address the court.

examinership: a statutory procedure whereby an examiner is appointed by the High Court for a short period to devise a scheme which either saves the company from liquidation or puts the company's affairs in order so as to facilitate a winding up.

execution of judgment: the process of enforcing the judgment of a court as against the unsuccessful party.

ex tempore: a judgment issued by a judge immediately after the evidence in a case has concluded.

fair procedures: the rules of procedure which must be applied by all courts, tribunals and persons exercising powers which affect another persons rights. The requirement is to give every party a proper hearing (*audi alteram parten*) and to be impartial and unbiased (*neino iudex in sua causa*).

felony: a crime which at one stage carried the death penalty. Contrasted with a misdemeanour which is a less serious offence and generally carries a lighter penalty. The distinction is not important today except that a person suspected of a felony can be arrested without warrant.

fiduciary: a special obligation or duty which falls on a person who is in control of the property of another. A fiduciary duty is strict and does not permit the person on whom the duty falls to be in a situation of conflict of interest or to profit secretly from his position. The directors of a company for example, have a fiduciary duty to the company.

fraudulent trading: any officer or servant of a company who is a party to the carrying on of a company's business with intent to defraud creditors is guilty of the criminal offence of fraudulent trading and in addition may be made personally liable for the company's debts and may also be the subject of a disqualification order.

garnishee order: where A is indebted to B and B is indebted to C as a result of a judgment in C's favour, C can apply to the court for a garnishee order directing A to pay C out of the monies which are owing by A to B.

guardian ad litem: a person appointed to safeguard the interests of a minor involved in litigation.

habeas corpus: where it appears to the High Court that a person is being detained in custody in a manner which is unconstitutional a habeas corpus order is made directing that the person be brought before the court and reasons given as to the grounds of his detention. If after legal argument the person is found to have been unconstitutionally detained he must then be freed by the court.

hearsay: evidence given by a witness which recites a statement made by another person. Hearsay evidence is generally inadmissible but there are a number of exceptions.

indictable offence: an offence for which the accused has the right to be tried by a jury. However the accused can and more often than not will exercise his right to be tried by a judge alone (known as summary trial) in the District Court where the maximum penalty is two years imprisonment.

indictment: a numbered list of charges against an accused person for which he is to be tried.

injunction: an order made by a court directing the taking of certain action by the defendant (a mandatory injunction) or the cessation of certain action (a prohibitory injunction) with the penalty of committal to prison for contempt of court in the event of failure to comply. In urgent cases an interim injunction can be obtained *ex parte* which will last for a short time whereupon the defendant can then challenge the injunction before the court. An interlocutory injunction if granted will last as long as it takes for the case to reach a full hearing. A judge will only grant an interlocutory injunction if satisfied that damages will not be an adequate remedy and that the balance of convenience favours the granting of the injunction.

inquisitorial procedure: criminal procedure adopted in civil law jurisdictions where the judge initiates the investigation and examines witnesses. The presumption of innocence as it applies in common law countries such as Ireland does not apply in such legal systems.

insanity: in criminal law the defence that a person was at the time when the offence was committed suffering from a mental illness such that (a) he was unable to determine the nature and quality of his act or that his act was wrong (the McNaughten Rules) or (b) he was unable to control his impulses (irresistible impulse). If the plea is successful the accused is detained in a criminal mental hospital until his release is ordered by the executive.

insider dealing: a criminal offence (punishable by prohibition from dealing for twelve months) and a civil wrong (rendering the person liable to any person involved in the deal who was not in possession of the information and liable to the company) committed by any person connected to a company who deals in securities (shares, stocks etc.) whilst in possession of information, which if known would materially affect the price of securities and which was not generally available to the public.

interlocutory: an application to the court by any party for relief before the close of pleadings and in advance of the trial date, *e.g.* an application for discovery or for an interlocutory injunction.

interrogatories: an interlocutory order (defused above) which directs a party to answer a series of questions raised by the other party the purpose of which is to narrow down the scope of the case being made by the party upon whom the interrogatories are served.

intestacy: where a person dies without making a will. There are specific rules governing the distribution of the assets of a deceased person.

Iris Oifigiúil: a twice weekly government publication wherein official notice is given of various matters of interest to the business community and the general public such as the appointment of receivers to companies or the striking off of companies *etc.*

judge's rules: a set of guidelines for members of the Garda Síochána regarding the interrogation of suspects in custody. A statement obtained from a suspect in custody in breach of the rules is admissible if it is proven to have been made voluntarily.

judgment: a decree or order of a court stating that a specified sum of money is owing by one party (the judgment debtor) to another party (the judgment creditor). The term is also used to describe a decision of a court on a particular case. (Note that this is the usual spelling when referring to legal matters).

judgment mortgage: the process whereby a judgment creditor (a person to whom money is owed on foot of a judgment in his favour against the judgment debtor) can convert his judgment into a mortgage against the judgment debtor's property. The judgment debtor will then be unable to sell the mortgaged property until the debt is paid.

judicial review: a procedure provided for in the rules of court whereby an application to the High Court is made (by a party known as the applicant) to challenge the finding or determination of an inferior court (District or Circuit) or tribunal or other person exercising a quasi judicial function (defined below). The grounds are that the respondent (the person who made the decision or determination) has acted beyond its jurisdiction (*i.e.* its lawful powers) or has failed to apply fair procedures. The applicant must apply *ex parte* in the judicial review list for leave to apply and if successful the respondent must then choose whether or not to show cause (defend or oppose the order).

judicial separation: a formal decree of a court relieving the parties of their marital obligations though not dissolving the marriage. Provision may also be made by the judge on maintenance of a spouse and children, custody of the children and the distribution or otherwise of the family home and other marital property.

Labour Court: a forum for the negotiation of industrial disputes set up by the Industrial Relations Act 1946. In addition to its role as a facilitator the Labour Court also adjudicates on appeals from the recommendations of equality officers under the Employment Equality Act 1977 and the Anti-Discrimination (Pay) Act 1974. From the finding of the Labour Court there is an appeal on a point of law only to the High Court.

labour injunction: an injunction to restrain a strike.

Labour Relations Commission (L.R.C.): a statutory body whose function is to promote and facilitate industrial relations. Most industrial disputes will be referred to the L.R.C. before the Labour Court becomes involved.

land registry: a government office under the department of justice which houses registers noting the ownership of land.

larceny: the criminal offence of theft. Often mistaken for robbery, larceny does not involve violence or force but relates to an intentional taking without consent with the intention of permanently depriving the owner of his propriety.

legal cost accountant: a professional person engaged by solicitors to advise on appropriate fees on individual cases and who will represent the solicitor before the Taxing Master (*q.v.*) here there is a dispute over fees.

lien: the right to hold the property of another until such time as that other pays a debt or performs a legal obligation which was due to the person exercising the lien, *e.g.* a mechanic keeping a car until its owner pays a repair bill.

liquidated damages: where the damages payable or a formula by which it is possible to calculate the damages payable in the event of a breach of a contract by either party are agreed in advance and form part of the contract.

liquidator: company law; a person appointed by the High Court (called an official liquidator) or by a company's members or creditor whose function is to collect and realise a company's assets, to pay off its debts, distribute any remaining assets to the company's members and to dissolve the company. A provisional liquidator is one appointed by a court in advance of a formal winding up application in circumstances where there is an urgency in relation to preserving the assets of the company.

locus standi: a plaintiff in an action must have a sufficient interest in the subject matter of the litigation in order to pursue the claim. If the plaintiff does not have sufficient interest he will not be entitled to proceed as he lacks *locus standi*.

lodgment: in a civil action a lodgment is a sum which a defendant pays into court which he considers to be adequate to compensate the plaintiff. The lodgment can be made with or without an admission of liability. The fact of a lodgment or its amount is not disclosed to the trial judge and if an award of damages is made to the plaintiff at the hearing which does not exceed the amount of the lodgment the defendant is entitled to his costs from the date the lodgment is made. (Note that this is the usual spelling when referring to legal matters).

long vacation: the months of July and August when the Circuit, High and Supreme Courts do not sit.

man of straw: a person who has no financial resources, who will not be a mark for damages or the recovery of legal costs.

mandamus: a form of relief sought by way of judicial review which commands an inferior court or tribunal or person exercising quasi-judicial power to act in accordance with its/his legal duties.

manslaughter: the criminal offence of unlawful killing but without malice aforethought or intent. Voluntary manslaughter is an intentional killing where the intent is vitiated by the provocation of the accused. Involuntary manslaughter is committed where a person is killed by the accused's unlawful act or recklessness.

Mareva injunction: *see* **injunction.**

Master of the High Court: a judicial officer of the High Court who sits in the Master's Court where various orders (*e.g.* Discovery) in relation to High Court civil litigation may be sought.

McNaghten Rules: *see* **insanity**

memorandum of association: *see* **company**

memorial: a summary of a deed which is lodged in the Registry of Deeds when a deed is being registered.

mens rea: the mental element of intention on the part of the accused which must generally be proven before the accused can be convicted.

minor offence: an offence which may be tried summarily, *i.e.* without a jury. Minor offences are tried in the District Court.

misdemeanour: *see* **felony.**

misdirection: an error on the part of a trial judge in instructing the jury on matters of law or evidence. In a civil case where a judge sits alone the judge must direct himself in the law and thus can also misdirect himself. A misdirection is a ground for appeal.

motion: an application to a judge seeking some form of relief in advance of the date of trial. Unless the rules of court provide for an application *ex parte* a motion must be notified in advance to the other side by way of notice of motion.

Motor Insurers Bureau of Ireland (M.I.B.I.): a company formed pursuant to agreement with the minister and funded by insurers who transact motor insurance business which deals with claims in respect of motor accidents caused by uninsured drivers, stolen vehicles and foreign registered vehicles.

murder: the unlawful killing of a person with malice aforethought which on conviction carries a mandatory life sentence.

natural justice: the requirement that a court or tribunal or person exercising quasi-judicial power apply fair procedures to all parties to a dispute or matter (*see* **fair procedures**).

natural law: law which is thought to emanate from god as contrasted with man-made or positive law.

negligence: a common law tort; where a person owes another a duty to take care and breaches that duty causing damage to that other person which flows from the breach of duty, the person causing the damage is liable to the injured party in negligence.

nemo iudex in causa sua: no man can be a judge in his own cause. A principle which requires a court, tribunal or administrative body or person to be impartial when deciding matters affecting the rights of persons (*see* **procedures**).

next friend: a person who pursues legal action on behalf of a minor. Usually a parent.

noble prosequi: where the prosecution in a criminal case withdraws before the conclusion of the case. The proceedings are then stayed but can be reactivated by the state at a later date.

notary public: a person, usually a solicitor appointed by the Chief Justice who is empowered to certify documents and deeds as authentic.

novus actus interveniens: an act of negligence which is committed by a third party after the original act of negligence of a defendant in a civil case which absolves the defendant of liability.

nuisance: a tort and in certain circumstances a crime which involves the unreasonable interference by a person with the rights of another. Public nuisance (which is a crime as well as a tort) is interference with the rights of the general public and only the Attorney General can sue unless a person can show particular damage over and above that sustained by the general public. Private nuisance is actionable by a private individual if he can show unreasonable interference with the enjoyment of his land.

nullity of marriage: a decree which declares that a valid marriage has never taken place or that if it has it has been rendered a nullity by reason of the occurrence of certain events such as the insanity of a spouse.

obiter dictum: a statement of law made by a judge in the course of a judgment which does not go to the root of the decision but which nonetheless can be quoted in a subsequent case as a persuasive but not a binding authority.

occupier's liability: the liability in tort of a person occupying (not necessarily owning) land to persons who are injured whilst on the land. The tort is now governed by the Occupiers Liability Act 1995 which provides for the classification of persons entering the land of another (entrants) in three categories: visitors, recreational users and trespassers with the strictest duty owed to the first category and lesser duties owed to the second and third.

partnership: the carrying on by two or more persons of a business in common with a view to making a profit.

passing off: the tort committed by a person who passes off his goods as those of another.

patent: an industrial property right whereby an idea, plan, concept process or product is protected and gives the patent holder the right to prevent all third parties from using the subject matter of the patent.

peace commissioner: a person appointed by order of the master for justice with responsibility for signing warrants and summonses and with the authority to administer oaths and declarations.

penal servitude: historically this sentence implied mandatory hard labour but nowadays there is no difference between such a sentence and one for imprisonment.

pleadings: formal legal documents used in civil proceedings the purpose of which is to identify and clarify the matters in issue between the parties. (see **civil bill, civil process, defence, plenary summons and statement of claim**).

plenary summons and statement of claim: a plenary summons is a document which initiates ordinary proceedings in the High Court. It contains only a brief statement of the relief sought by the plaintiff and is followed by a more elaborate description of the plaintiff's case contained in a statement of claim.

precedent: a report or judgment from a previous case which is cited or quoted to a judge in support of a legal argument.

preferential creditor: a creditor of a company, a bankrupt or a deceased person who is entitled by statute to rank higher than ordinary creditors in the queue for payment out of the assets available.

preliminary examination: an enquiry carried out in the District Court as to the evidence against an accused before he is sent forward for trial by jury.

private law: the law dealing with civil disputes between private citizens or companies and not usually involving the state, *e.g.* tort, contract *etc.*

private international law: the body of law dealing with relations and disputes between private citizens or companies of different countries.

privilege: (1) the right not to produce documents for discovery on the basis that they contain information which should not be disclosed to the other party for reasons of fairness or public policy; (2) a defence to a claim for defamation which admits the statement made and that it was defamatory but asserts the rights of the defendant to make the statement under various categories of exceptional circumstances recognised by law. Such a privilege can be absolute or qualified and if qualified the protection of the privilege will be lost if the plaintiff can show malice on the part of the defendant.

probate: a general term to describe the legal distribution of the assets of a deceased person.

product liability: the civil liability falling on the retailer, manufacturer, producer, importer, distributor *etc.* for damage or injury caused by a defect in a product (generally including a service) supplied by that person. Now covered by the Liability for Defective Products Act 1991.

promoter: a person who takes it upon himself to set up a company. Promoters have a fiduciary duty to the company.

public law: constitutional law, criminal law and administrative law. That body of law which deals with the relations between the state and citizens.

quasi-judicial: a process or power or function the exercise of which requires the person presiding to exercise his/her/its power in a judicial manner. This means that fair procedures must be applied before a decision is taken.

quia timet: a form of legal order granted to prevent an anticipated wrongful act by another, *e.g.* a Mareva injunction, an anton piller injunction.

rape: unlawful sexual intercourse, penetration of the anus or mouth by the penis, penetration of the vagina by an object. Criminal Law (Rape) (Amendment Act) 1990.

ratio decidendi: the precise legal basis for a court's decision in a previous case. Binding as a precedent on a lower court unless it can be distinguished from the facts of the subsequent case or can be shown to be erroneous (*see* **precedent, obiter dicta**).

receiver: a person appointed to take charge of a company's assets or part thereof with a view to paying of a debt owed to a particular creditor. A receiver has no power to wind up a company.

recklessness: an act of gross carelessness falling just short of an intentional act.

reckless trading: a statutory civil liability in company law whereby any officer of the company was responsible for carrying on business or for involving the company in a transaction which was likely to cause loss to the company's creditors.

recognisance: a promise made to a court to do a certain thing, *e.g.* to appear in court on a particular date.

recreational user: a category of entrant onto a persons land (*see* **Occupiers Liability Act 1995**).

regulation: a piece of E.C. legislation which is binding on all member states without the need for national legislation to implement it into a Member States' law.

remand: the sending back of an accused person (either in custody or on bail) to appear in court on a later date.

re ipsa loquitur: a rule of evidence which presumes that certain accidents could not happen in the absence of negligence. Once the rule is found to apply to a defendant's conduct the onus of proof shifts to him to prove that he was not negligent.

res judicata: a legal argument seeking to end proceedings on the basis that the same issue between the same parties has been decided already by another court.

rescission: the setting aside of a contract on equitable grounds and the restoration of the parties to the position they occupied prior to entering into the contract (restitution).

reserved judgment: a judgment which is delivered in open court some time (but not immediately) after the conclusion of the hearing of a case.

restriction order: an order made by the High Court in company law matters against an officer or servant of a company which is insolvent and in liquidation where the officer or servant has been irresponsible in his handling of a company's affairs. The order restricts the activities of that person for a specified time in relation to the management of the affairs of any other company.

Rights Commissioner: a statutory officer appointed by the Labour Relations Commission responsible for the investigation of and adjudication on individual grievances relating to employment. A right of appeal exists to the Employment Appeals Tribunal.

robbery: an act of larceny involving violence to the victim or the perception by the victim of a threat of violence.

Rylands v. Fletcher, the Rule in: the common law tort whereby a landowner is made responsible for loss or damage sustained as a result of the escape from his premises of a dangerous thing or substance which he has brought onto or collected on his premises.

safety statement: a statement dealing with hazards and precautions in the workplace which must be drafted with the co-operation of employees and displayed at the place of work or otherwise communicated to employees.

scheduled offence: an offence declared by the government to be one which is triable in the Special Criminal Court and to which the powers of arrest and detention conferred by section 30 of the Offences Against the State Act 1939 apply.

sequestration: a special type of order resulting from contempt of court whereby a person's assets are seized until he has complied with the court order.

seriatim: one by one in order, *e.g.* a defence can traverse (deny) a series of allegations in a statement of claim *seriatim*.

shadow director: a person who though not a director is capable of exerting a controlling influence on a company.

sheriff: a court officer whose principal function is to oversea the execution of judgments by taking possession of a debtor's assets.

specific performance: an equitable remedy which forces a party in breach of contract to carry out his obligations under the contract.

Statute of Frauds 1695: an Act which requires certain contracts to be reduced to writing before they will be legally enforceable.

Statute of Limitations: a period prescribed by statute within which a civil claim must be initiated.

Statutory Declaration: a sworn written statement usually declaring that a certain state of affairs exists, *e.g.* that a house is not a family home.

strict liability: liability in tort which is established without proof of fault on the part of the person found liable, *e.g.* nuisance, *Rylands v. Fletcher.*

subpoena: (called a witness summons if issued by the Circuit or District Courts): a document summoning a person to court at a particular date and time to give evidence and sometimes to bring documents as well. A witness failing to appear can be jailed for contempt.

Journalists and the Law

subrogation: the right of one person to "stand in the shoes" of a second person and so enforce rights against a third party normally only exercisable by the second person.

substantive: pertaining to the actual substance of a particular dispute rather than to the procedure by which the dispute is to be heard.

summary: used in various contexts but usually meaning a legal process which is shortened by cutting out an element of the procedure, *e.g.* summary trial cuts out a jury, summary dismissal is dismissal without notice, summary judgment is judgment without contest by the defendant, summary proceedings are heard without oral evidence and affidavits are used instead.

summons: the method of iniation of certain (usually minor) criminal proceedings in the District Court.

surety: a person into whose charge an accused person is released on bail. The surety will also usually post a bail bond which is forfeited if the accused fails to appear.

taxation of costs/Taxing Master: where an award of costs is made against an unsuccessful party and that party disputes the amount of the costs he is being asked to pay the dispute will be referred to the Taxing Master for adjudication if the case was in the High Court or to the County Registrar or District Court Registrar if the case was heard in those courts. Prior to submitting the costs the solicitor will refer his file to a costs drawer or legal costs accountant who will provide specialist advice on the appropriate fee. The cost drawer will also usually represent the solicitor in the Taxing Master's Court.

testimony: oral evidence given by a witness in court.

trade union: the most common and most important is a registered trade union which is the only type of trade union which benefits from statutory immunity in tort (*see* **conspiracy**). A registered trade union holds a licence to negotiate on behalf of its members and must post a bond with the Registrar of Friendly Societies. The rules relating to companies are analogous to those regulating trade unions.

transfer of undertaking: where a business is taken over as a going concern by another business E.C. law protects the employees of the business from compulsory redundancy.

trespasser: a person who enters the land of another without permission or who enters initially with permission but then engages in an unlawful activity. The duty of care owed to a trespasser by an occupier of land is merely not to intentionally or recklessly injure him (*see* **Occupiers Liability Act 1995**).

trust: an equitable concept where a person known as a trustee holds property for the benefit of another person or persons called a *cestui qui* trust.

uberrimae fidei: utmost good faith: a principle applying to some contracts especially insurance contracts where both parties have an obligation to disclose to each other all matters relevant to the contract. The opposite of *caveat emptor* where it is up to the buyer to make full enquiry and the seller is not obliged to disclose matters relevant to the contract which the buyer could discover for himself.

ultra vires: in company law where a company engages in an activity which is beyond the scope of the objects of that company as stated in its memorandum of association it is acting *ultra vires* and any contract entered into by the company in pursuance of such an *ultra vires* activity is void. In administrative law an administrative body or person with delegated authority acts *ultra vires* when it goes beyond the terms of reference of the delegated power conferred.

volenti non fit injuria: a defence to a claim in negligence to the effect that the plaintiff voluntarily brought the risk of injury upon himself.

voluntary liquidation: a liquidation iniated by a company's members or creditors where the liquidator is appointed by the creditors or members but not by the court. Unlike a compulsory liquidation there is no direct court supervision of the procedure.

visitor: a category of entrant onto the land of another under the Occupiers Liability Act 1995.

without prejudice: a form of privilege over a written or oral communication where it is understood that the details of the communication will not be disclosed to a court.

writ: civil legal proceedings.

1. THE COURTS

The Constitution provides for the administration of justice in public, in courts established by law, by judges appointed in the manner provided by the Constitution. The important pieces of legislation giving effect to this are:

1. The Courts (Establishment and Constitution) Act 1961,

2. The Courts (Supplemental Provisions) Act 1961,

3. The Courts and Court Officers Act 1995.

THE JURISDICTION OF THE COURTS

The jurisdiction of a court means the power of a court to hear and decide a case. The work of the courts is divided between its criminal and its civil jurisdiction.

Criminal Jurisdiction

Article 38 of the Constitution provides that no person shall be tried on any criminal charge save in due course of law and that, with three exceptions, no person shall be tried on a criminal charge without a jury. The exceptions are:

1. minor offences which may be tried by courts of summary jurisdiction, *i.e.* the District Court;

2. Special courts, like the Special Criminal Court, may be established to try cases where it has been decided that the ordinary courts are inadequate to secure the administration of justice and the preservation of public peace and order; and

3. Military Tribunals may be established for the trials of offences against military law and also to deal with a state of war or armed rebellion.

The District Court

The criminal jurisdiction of the District Court is divided in two. First of all it acts as a clearing house for serious crime through its preliminary examination procedure. Secondly it hears all minor offences. In the District Court a judge sits alone without a jury.

Minor offences   The kinds of offences which the District Court hears include road traffic offences, public disorder offences, minor thefts, assaults and minor drug offences. The penalty it can impose is limited to 12 months imprisonment with a total of up to two years for multiple offences. When hearing cases of this kind the court is said to be using its summary jurisdiction.

Other offences   Some more serious crimes, known as indictable offences, can be tried in the District Court. The court must be satisfied that the facts proved or alleged constitute a minor offence, and the accused person, having been informed of his right to trial by jury, opts for trial by the District Court. In certain cases the Director of Public Prosecutions must consent to the matter being heard in the District Court. The main effect from the accused's point of view of having the matter disposed of in the District Court is that the court is restricted in the penalty it can impose.

Preliminary Investigation   Because of the growth in serious crime a good deal of the District Court's time is taken up with the preliminary investigation process. When a person is charged with a serious crime which for one reason or another cannot be disposed of in the District Court, and will have to be tried by a higher court, the judge can remand the accused while the State's case is being prepared. This preparation takes the form of assembling what is known as a book of evidence which is served on the accused.

There are time limits within which the book should be served but they are more observed in the breach. If a District Judge feels the remand period is being abused he can strike out the charges.

The book of evidence consists of a statement of the charges, the list of witnesses whom it is proposed to call, statements of their evidence and a list of the exhibits it is proposed to use at the trial. After this is served on the accused a preliminary examination must be conducted by the District Judge to satisfy himself that the accused has a case to answer. Only when this is done does the the judge send the matter forward for trial. In practice the accused often waives the preliminary examination.

Procedure in summary matters The usual procedure adopted by the District Court in summary matters is that following an application a summons is served on the accused indicating the nature of the offence and its time and place of commission and requiring the attendance in court of the accused to answer the charges. The accused can seek the statements of witnesses prior to the trial of the case.[1] If the defendant has been arrested and brought to court the procedure is by charge sheet.

The Circuit Court

Indictable offences The Circuit Court has original jurisdiction in relation to indictable offences except for treason, murder, attempted or conspiracy to murder, piracy, rape, certain serious offences under the Treason Act of 1939 and the Offences Against the State Act of 1939. The trial will normally take place in front of a judge sitting with a jury on the circuit on which the offence has been committed or where the accused person has been arrested or resides. Under the Court and Court Officers Act 1995, where an accused person has been sent forward for trial to a Circuit Court sitting other than in the Dublin Circuit Court, the judge of the Circuit Court before whom the accused is triable may on the application of the prosecutor or the accused, if satisfied that it would be manifestly unjust not to do so, transfer the trial to the Circuit Court sitting within the Dublin circuit. The Circuit Court judge's decision in this instance to grant or refuse the application is final and unappealable.

The indictment When an accused person is sent forward for trial the prosecution must prepare an indictment. This document sets out the formal charge which the Director of Public Prosecutions or in certain instances the Attorney General prefers against the accused.

---

[1] *Cowzer v. Kirby*, unreported, High Court, Barr J., February 2, 1991.

The arraignment The next stage in the process is the arraignment. By this is meant the accused is brought before the Circuit Court and the charges against him as set out in the indictment are read out to him and he is asked whether he wishes to plead guilty or not guilty. Remember he and his lawyers will already know the state's case against him from the book of evidence. If the state decide that they are not proceeding with the trial they will normally enter a *nolle prosequi* at this stage.

Plea bargaining If the case is planned to continue there may be an opportunity for the defendant through his counsel to plea bargain in relation to the offences with which he is charged. Literally what is meant by plea bargaining is that the accused is unwilling to plead to the charges as set out in the indictment but may be willing to plead to a lesser charge or to a number of charges set out in the indictment. Although plea bargaining is more formalised in countries like the United States of America, it is nevertheless a feature of the Irish system although conducted on a much more informal level.

   If the accused pleads not guilty to the charges then a jury has to be empanelled.

Selection of a jury Suitability for jury service is now decided by the Juries Act 1976. Subject to that Act, every citizen aged 18 years and upwards and under the age of 70 years who is entered in the Dáil Register of Electors in a particular jury district is qualified. A person is liable to serve if called upon unless at the time they are called they are ineligible or disqualified. Persons who would be deemed ineligible include the President of Ireland, people concerned with the administration of justice, *i.e.* a practising barrister or a solicitor, members of An Garda Síochána and prison and welfare officers, members of the defence forces and persons who are illiterate or deaf or mental patients. In addition people can be disqualified for jury service, if for example, they have been convicted of a criminal offence attracting a certain type of prison sentence. There is also a process whereby people may be excused from jury service. Those excused by right would be those who served on a jury within the past three years or those who may be excused at the discretion of the County Registrar of the court and among that group would be people like medical practitioners who cannot be spared from certain jobs. If a person gets ill they can apply to be excused from jury service but if summoned to attend a person must attend unless excused, disqualified or ineligible.

The ballot Usually the 12 people selected to serve on any particular jury are selected by ballot in open court. Literally, the County Registrar puts all the numbers of those called for jury service on a particular day into a bag and picks them out at random. Both the prosecution and the defence have a right to object to a particular jury member. Two forms of objection can be taken , one peremptory which means that no cause has to be shown as to why either side do not want that particular juror serving on the jury. Both the prosecution and the defence have seven challenges of this sort and once their respective challenges have been exhausted they can then challenge further members of the jury provided they can show cause. In practice this is rarely done although both the prosecution and the defence usually use up their peremptory challenges.

The verdict Once the jury is sworn in the trial proceeds and results in an acquittal or a conviction. There can also be a direction. If, at the end of the prosecution's case, an application is made to the judge that based on the evidence given, there is no case to answer then the judge may direct the jury as a matter of law to find the accused not guilty or he may refuse to grant such a direction.

Appellate jurisdiction of the Circuit Court The other main area of work with which the Circuit Court deals is appeals from the District Court. Such appeals take the form of a complete re-hearing and it is open to the accused to call new evidence if he wishes. The Circuit Court can vary any sentence imposed in the District Court and it also has the power to increase the penalty imposed.

The Central Criminal Court

The High Court exercising its criminal jurisdiction is known as the Central Criminal Court and it sits in Dublin. It has exclusive jurisdiction in relation to such areas as murder, attempted murder, rape and normally tries these cases in a similar manner to the procedure in the Circuit Court.

The Court of Criminal Appeal

The Court of Criminal Appeal comprises three judges, one of which must be the Chief Justice or an ordinary judge of the Supreme Court nominated and the other two judges must be from the High Court. The Court of Criminal Appeal's jurisdiction is to hear appeals from the Central Criminal Court, the Circuit Court and the Special Criminal Court.

The Special Criminal Court

The Offences Against the State Act 1939 which provides for the establishment of the Special criminal Court may be brought into force whenever the government is satisfied that the ordinary courts are inadequate to secure the effective administration of justice and the preservation of public peace and order. Two challenges were made to the constitutionality of the court but its validity was upheld, particularly by the Supreme Court in *Re McCurtain*.[2] Three members comprise the court but no person can be appointed unless he is a judge of the High Court, the Circuit Court or the District Court, a barrister or a solicitor of not less than seven years standing or an officer of the defence forces not below the rank of commandant. In practice the court usually comprises a combination of those holding judicial office. The court sits without a jury.

Military Courts

The system also provides for the establishment of military courts, called courts martial. The jurisdiction is to try people for an offence against military law committed by such a person whilst subject to military law as an officer or man. Membership of the court is confined to officers of the Defence forces, not less than five in the case of a general Court Martial and three in the case of a limited Court Martial.

The Supreme Court

An appeal from the Court of Criminal Appeal may lie to the Supreme

---

[2] [1941] I.R. 83.

Court if the Attorney General or the Court of Criminal Appeal certifies that the decision involves a point of law of exceptional public importance that it is desirable in the public interest that the opinion of the Supreme Court be taken. In additional an appeal lies directly from the Central Criminal Court against interlocutory orders such as appeal pending trial or costs. There are other appeals to the Supreme Court, the most interesting being an appeal to the Supreme Court from the High Court on a case stated from the District Court once leave to appeal has been obtained from the High Court.

CIVIL JURISDICTION

While undoubtedly the criminal courts provide constant copy for journalists of all sorts, cases within the civil area are now beginning to be covered quite intensively particularly by those in the print area. Procedure plays an important role in the running of the civil cases before the Irish courts. There are complex sets of rules and regulations which govern civil proceedings. The Rules of the Superior Courts were revised in 1986 and govern the procedure in the High Court and the Supreme Court. Similarly there are rules for the District Court and rules for the Circuit Court. In all cases the rules are subject to ongoing scrutiny and revision and are supplemented by what are known as practice directives. These are directives which judges issue to attempt to make the system run more efficiently.

In considering the civil jurisdiction of the courts, it is important to bear in mind that the vast majority of cases settle without going into court at all. Some cases settle once an initiating letter has been written by a solicitor to the other side whereas others take some time longer to settle.

Small Claims Court

A new initiative which has been started in recent years is the introduction of Small Claims Courts. These courts are run out of the District Court offices. They deal with claims of up to £600. In order to avail of the service both sides must be agreeable in advance to be bound by the findings of the court.

The District Court

The main areas of civil jurisdiction for the District Court are:

General Cases of contract and tort and cases of ejectment and in cases of ejectment for non-payment of rent the court can award damages not exceeding £5,000. Excluded from those areas are defamation, false imprisonment and malicious prosecution which must be taken in a higher court.

Family Law Under the huge volume of family law legislation passed in the last 20 years, the District Court plays a major role in areas dealing in the main with maintenance, custody and barring orders. Again, it is precluded from granting a decree of judicial separation and it is not anticipated it will be able to grant a divorce decree when the new legislation is enacted.

Licensing Another major area covered by the District Court relates to licensing matters. The court deals with objections to the renewal of a licence.

Miscellaneous There are other areas covered by the civil jurisdiction of the District Court such as hire purchase claims.

Finally, it should be noted that the District Court is presided over by a judge sitting alone and anyone dissatisfied with the decision of the District Court can appeal to the Circuit Court.

The Circuit Court

The Circuit Court, like the District Court, is presided over by a judge alone and is a court of record. Like the District Court it is an extremely busy court when exercising its civil jurisdiction.

General It deals with a wide range of cases in the tort and contract areas. For example, actions for defamation, false imprisonment and malicious prosecution can be taken in the Circuit Court. The main restriction on the court is that in general it cannot award more than £30,000 damages. If both parties to an action consent then it can have unlimited jurisdiction but this rarely happens.

Land It can resolve any matter relating to land where the rateable valuation is under £200.

Landlord and Tenant Another major area dealt with by the Circuit Court is cases relating to the granting of new leases and those covered by the Landlord and Tenant (Amendment) Act 1980.

Equity Suits Here again the court has the ability to deal with a wide range of equity matters, *e.g.* injunctions with a special proviso that the rateable valuation of the does not exceed £200.

Family Law Under the Judicial Separation and Family Law Act 1989 and the Family Law Act of 1995 the Circuit Court is the main court dealing with all family law matters. When exercising its jurisdiction it is known as the family court and it can deal with judicial separation and all the consequential orders that arise from a judicial separation and since the enactment of the 1995 Act can now deal with nullity cases. There has been enormous growth in this particular area of the court's work in the past 10 years and because of lengthy delays, particularly in the Dublin area, a number of new judges were appointed in the summer of 1996 to alleviate the problem.

Licensing matters The court can grant new licences or declaratory orders that premises are suitable to be licensed. It also deals with the granting of new restaurant licences.

Appellate jurisdiction of the Circuit Court The Circuit Court also deals with civil appeals from the District Court which are by way of a full re-hearing. The Circuit Court deals with appeals from the Employment Appeals Tribunal.

The High Court

Under our Constitution the High Court has original jurisdiction to determine all matters and questions whether of law or fact, civil and criminal. Since the Courts Act 1988, juries sit in the High Court only to determine actions for defamation, false imprisonment and malicious prosecution. Before that they heard all personal injuries cases. In practice the work of the High Court is divided into a number of areas:

Personal injuries litigation There is no limit on the amount of damages which the High Court can involve in a personal injuries case. A great deal of the work of the High Court is taken up with the hearing of such cases. The court also deals with any contract case which is worth more than £15,000.

Chancery Another major wing of the High Court deals with chancery matters.

Companies and Bankrupty Under the Companies Act 1963 and the Bankruptcy Act 1988 the High Court has exclusive jurisdiction in both of these areas.

Constitutional areas Another area of exclusivity to the High Court is the determination of the constitutional validity of legislation.

Stateside proceedings A major growth area for the High Court in the last 10 years has been stateside proceedings. Individuals or bodies seek orders of *certiorari*, habeas corpus, mandamus against decision-makers of all kinds.

The Supreme Court

Matters decided in the High Court can be appealed to the Supreme Court but the appeal does not take the form of a full re-hearing of the case. Most appeals are limited to points of law. In addition the Supreme Court, under Article 26 of the Constitution, can decide on the constitutionality of any proposed new legislation. These matters are referred to it by the President after consultation with the Council of State.

The European Court of Justice

The European Court of Justice is part of the European Community which adjudicates upon the law in the Community and its rulings are binding on the Irish courts.

The European Court of Human Rights

The European Court of Human Rights is part of the Council of Europe and it investigates breaches of the European Convention of

Human Rights. It is in Strasbourg and its decisions are not binding. The significance of the European court will be dealt with from a journalistic perspective later.

Judicial and Quasi-Judicial Bodies

There are a range of tribunals and other judicial and quasi-judicial bodies that will deal with specialist legal problems. This chapter deals with only a number of them because The list is quite exhaustive and what has been selected here are the more common ones which the media are likely to cover in the course of a day's work. While these bodies are not courts within the meaning of Article 34 of the Constitution, they nevertheless have to act judicially and must hear all sides of a case and are subject to judicial review in the High Court if they fail to act correctly.

Employment Appeals Tribunal The Employment Appeals Tribunal (EAT) was set up under section 18 of the Unfair Dismissals Act 1977. In the main it deals with unfair dismissal cases. It can also deal with disputes relating to minimum notice, maternity protection and redundancy. A typical tribunal will comprise the Chairperson who is a lawyer, either a solicitor or barrister and a representative nominated by the Irish Congress of Trade Unions and one nominated by the employers' organisation IBEC.

A person dismissed from their job can refer the issue of the dismissal to a rights commissioner who will deal with the matter in an informal way but it is more usual for the matter to be referred directly to the EAT. While the headquarters of the tribunal is situated in Dublin, divisions of the tribunal travel throughout the country to hear cases at different venues. Section 66 of the Unfair Dismissals Act 1977 places the burden of proving the fairness of a dismissal on an employer. If there is a dispute about the fact of dismissal then the employee has the burden of proof. The hearings of the EAT are generally in public. The tribunal usually reserves its decision and the reasons and conclusions are provided to the press in written form if there is a request to do so. Each side bears its own costs for the tribunal but the finding of a tribunal can be appealed to the Circuit Court which can award costs to one side or the other. This decision in turn can be appealed on a point of law to the High Court.

Coroner's Court The Coroner's Act 1962 prescribes the procedure under which an inquest must be held and in which a coroner's jury must be summoned to issue a verdict on the death of a person. It is severely limited by the Act to what it may or may not decide. No decision can be given which would in any way implicate the person in a criminal law sense, nor can the court decide to make a finding of unlawful killing. A controversial area which it cannot deal with is the question of bringing in a verdict of suicide.

The Coroner's Court is provided over by either a lawyer or a person with medical qualification and often by a person who possesses both qualifications.

Criminal Injuries Compensation Tribunal This tribunal was established by a scheme which was introduced by the government in 1974 but it has been amended many times since. Once again the tribunal comprises three persons, either barristers or solicitors. Prior to 1986 a person who was injured as a result of a criminal act could apply to the tribunal for compensation. Since that date the tribunal only has the power to award special damages as a result of a criminal act. There is provision for compensation to be paid where the injuries result from a riot or from the activities of an illegal organisation.

Tribunal of Enquiries The Tribunal of Enquiries (Evidence) Acts 1921 and 1979 enabled the government to establish tribunals of enquiry to investigate matters that pose difficulty for the Oireachtas. The most famous one in recent years was the Beef Tribunal and more recently the Tribunal of Enquiry into the activities of the Blood Bank. The tribunal has powers similar to a court of law and is generally speaking chaired by a High Court or Supreme Court judge. Tribunals of Enquiry can make recommendations but its findings are not binding on a court of law.

Planning Appeals Board This body was established by Local Government Planning and Development Act (1976) and it hears appeals from either the granting or the refusal of planning permission. The Board comprises five members and a chairman and all the positions are full-time. Most of the appeals are dealt with by way of written submission but there will be occasional public hearings which are generally presided over by an inspector who reports back to the Board who then take the decision on the appeal.

2. THE LEGAL PROFESSION

In Ireland the legal profession is divided into two main branches; solicitors and barristers.

Solicitors

Solicitors deal directly with clients and handle all sorts of legal business. The profession is governed by the Law Society of Ireland. Until recently, a law degree was required for admission to the profession but that was changed by a High Court decision.[1] At present, entrance is by way of an examination of degree standard. Following admission, students must undertake and complete a number of practical courses provided by the Law Society as well as working in an office before qualifying. During an apprenticeship the student is paid a nominal amount and works in the office where they are apprenticed. Until recently solicitors have tended not to exercise the right of audience in the Circuit and High Courts. Now, especially in country areas, it is notable that solicitors are handling cases in the Circuit Court, more in the area of District Court Appeals than Circuit Court cases proper. While it may well happen in the future, we do not, as yet, have solicitor advocates as in Scotland. In former times the work of a solicitor and a barrister was quite distinct but more recently that distinction has become somewhat blurred. The solicitor was always seen as the person who prepared the case for the barrister to advocate in court and who traditionally spent a good deal of time in the office working on conveyancing, wills, probate and preparing cases for litigation. Today, with the rise in new types of law, for example family law and employment law, solicitors are as qualified as barristers to litigate these matters and in some cases have taken on that responsibility. Apart from a handful of solicitors, advocacy in the higher courts tends to be the preserve of the Bar.

Qualified solicitors can become commissioners for oaths and notaries public.

---

[1] *Bloomer v. Incorporated Law Society, Irish Times Law Reports*, November 6, 1995.

The President of the High Court is responsible for the professional conduct of solicitors. The Law Society investigates any allegation of misconduct by a solicitor and can impose various penalties on the solicitor up to and including applying to the President of the High Court to have the solicitor struck off the rolls. This means that the solicitor can no longer practice as a solicitor.

All solicitors carry compulsory Professional Indemnity Insurance. This means that if a solicitor acts negligently his clients can take comfort in the fact that proper compensation will be paid.

The Law Society has stringent controls for ensuring that solicitors do not in any way mishandle their clients' money. The Law Society operates a compensation fund into which each solicitor pays to ensure that if a solicitor does defraud a client, the client will be refunded their money.

The introduction of lay persons on various committees dealing with solicitors' misconduct has insured that all client complaints are now thoroughly investigated by the Society.

The rules governing the conduct of solicitors are contained in the Solicitors Acts 1954, 1960 and 1994.

Barristers

Barristers are known collectively as the "Bar" and also as "Counsel". The term derives from an old practice where barristers practised at the "bar" of the court. originally the bar was a partition separating the judges from the ordinary person attending court but all that distinction is now gone and only the term barrister has survived. A barrister will generally get his work from a solicitor. In recent times there is limited direct access from other professions such as accountants and surveyors. When a barrister is given work by a solicitor it is termed "briefing" a barrister. Traditionally barristers wore wigs and gowns when they were conducting a case in court but since the introduction of the Court and Court Officers Act of 1995 the wearing of the wig is optional. In courts dealing with family law matters, the wearing of the wig and gown is prohibited. When a barrister is practising at the Bar for ten years or more he can apply to the Government to become a senior counsel or "Silk" which entitles him to use the words Senior Council (SC) after his name as opposed to junior counsel who use the letters BL. A senior counsel will wear a gown of silk rather than cotton in his practice. It is also the practice for clients with relatively serious cases to employ the services of a senior counsel, in addition to a junior counsel.

Before embarking on a practice at the Bar it is necessary to become a student of the King's Inns. The King's Inns offers a diploma course in law and a degree course in law – each course runs for two years. It is an unusual academic institution in that students who are in other jobs can pursue a law course because most of the lectures are held in late afternoon, evenings and on Saturday mornings. The most direct route is to gain entry into the degree course but to do that you must have a very good honours degree in law from a university or similar institution.

People without a legal degree will opt for the diploma course and again as numbers are limited the standards of entry are constantly rising and a good honours degree in a discipline other than law may be required to gain admission to the diploma course. There is some degree of flexibility in that if a person has worked in a legal or quasi-legal position this can be taken into account when applying for a diploma place. Successful completion of the diploma course does not necessarily guarantee a place on the degree course. The numbers for entry into the degree course are limited and only approximately 50 per cent of the places are reserved for diploma graduates.

Discipline within the Bar

Complaints of misconduct against barristers are investigated and adjudicated upon by the Barristers Professional Conduct Tribunal. The Tribunal consists of seven members, five of whom are practising barristers appointed by the Bar Council and two lay people, one nominated by IBEC and the other by the ICTU.

Other Training

Other training in the legal area is provided by the universities and by private colleges. One course which is outside the ambit of both of these structures is the course provided by the Dublin Vocational Education Committee. It provides a part-time diploma in legal studies and is a much sought after qualification because of the success rate of its students in obtaining places in the Incorporated Law Society and the diploma course in King's Inns. A university degree which at one stage did guarantee a place in the Law Society no longer does so. The private colleges in the main tend to opt for conferring on their students a degree from a British university.

The Judiciary

1996 saw one of the great expansions of the judiciary in Ireland. The Court and Court Officers Act 1995 provided for a substantial increase in the number of judges involved in the administration of justice and also brought about minor changes in the method of appointment and provided for the training of judges.

The Supreme Court

The Supreme Court comprises the Chief Justice and seven ordinary judges who are known as Judges of the Supreme Court. For the first time in its history the Supreme Court may sit in two or more divisions and they may sit at the same time.

The High Court, Circuit and District

There are 20 High Court judges (one of whom is the President of the High Court), 24 Circuit Court judges (one of whom is the President of the Circuit Court) and 48 District Court judges (one of whom is the President of the District Court).

Judicial appointments

The main change introduced by the 1995 Act was the establishment of what is known as the Judicial Appointments Advisory Board. The Board consists of:

1. The Chief Justice;

2. The President of the High Court;

3. The President of the Circuit Court;

4. The President of the District Court;

5. The Attorney General;

6. A practising barrister nominated by the Chairman of the Bar Council;

7. A practising solicitor nominated by the President of the Law Society;

8. Not more than three ordinary lay people appointed by the Minister for Justice.

Establishment of the board has led to advertisements being placed for judicial appointments and applicants interested in the post are required to complete an application form. The board considers the application and sends forward the names of suitable personnel to the Government who then select from the names put forward those they consider suitable and advise the President who actually appoints judicial personnel.

Qualification of judges

Two major changes introduced by the 1995 Act in relation to the appointment of judges was the ability to take into account service in the European Court, either as a judge of the Court of Justice, a judge of the Court of First Instance or as an advocate general. Taking the totality of such service or amalgamating such service with practice at the Bar the person seeking the appointment must be able to show at least 12 years standing for an appointment of the Supreme or the High Court. Another change saw the introduction of practising solicitors of not less than 10 years standing being eligible on the same basis as practising barristers of similar standing to appointment to the Circuit and the District Courts. Judges are appointed for life and can only be removed for stated misbehaviour and incapacity and then only on a resolution passed by both Houses of the Oireachtas.

Judicial salaries

Judicial salaries which are set in accordance with civil service guidelines, currently stand at:

Supreme Court Judge:	£87,051
High Court Judge:	£80,179
Circuit Court Judge:	£59,562
District Court Judge:	£49,254

Court Sittings

The sittings of the courts are determined by statute but basically the legal year is divided into four terms. The Hilary term starts in January and usually runs through to March. The Easter term follows that, starting after Easter week until just before Whit Sunday Trinity term starts sometime after Whitsun until July 31 and the Michaelmas term starts on the first Monday of October until December 21. No formal change has been made in these terms but because the business of the courts has increased substantially over the past decade, judges are available during the vacation periods to hear applications. Some judges who are in the course of hearing a lengthy case will require everybody in attendance during the vacation periods so that the conduct of the case can be expedited.

Director of Public Prosecutions

The Director of Public Prosecutions is appointed by the government to advise on matters of criminal law. He heads up the State prosecution service and is completely independent in his functions.

Attorney General

The Attorney General is the legal adviser to the government. He is appointed to the government and will sit at the Cabinet table. He may or may not be a T.D. The policy in recent years has been to appoint a senior barrister although it is possible now for a solicitor to be appointed to the office of Attorney General. The Attorney General has the option of representing the government on serious legal cases involving the government.

Other Court Officers

A number of other court officers need to be mentioned.

The Master of the High Court

The Master of the High Court is authorised by law to exercise limited functions and powers of a judicial nature within the scope of Article 37 of Constitution. He sits in the Four Courts and he deals with a wide range of motions that assist in the orderly conduct of the case. He cannot rule on any dispute or fact and must send that matter forward to the High Court. His orders can be appealed to the High Court.

The Taxing Master

The Taxing Master of the High Court deals effectively with any dispute relating to the costs of a particular action. He too sits in the Four Courts and his decisions are appealable to the High Court.

County Registrar

Each county has a County Registrar who is responsible for the administration of the Circuit Court and who under the 1995 Act has been given wide-ranging powers. His powers which are set out in schedule two of the Court and Courts Officers Act of 1995 are not too dissimilar to the Master of the High Court except that he can with the consent of all parties assess damages and with the consent of all parties try any issue of fact. In practical terms the county registrar is a person with whom journalists, particularly local reporters, will have contact and it is not uncommon to see a reporter sharing the same bench as the county registrar at the Circuit Court level.

Court Registrars

Another important element in the administration of the courts is the role played by the High Court Registrars. Each High Court judge will have sitting with them a Court Registrar. Again from a journalist's point of view the court registrar can be of invaluable assistance particularly if the case is of a technical nature.

Finding out what goes on in the courts

Each day a list is published indicating cases listed for that particular day and also giving advance warning of cases that are likely to be heard in the future. This is called *The Legal Diary*. Newspapers or individuals can subscribe to it, and it is posted up early in the Round Hall of the Four Courts. This list indicates in what courts the matters are going to be heard and who is likely to hear the case. It also provides information on motions that are before the courts, appeals and in Dublin covers not only the High Court but also the Circuit Court, both criminal and civil. Outside Dublin journalists have to rely on the various Circuit and District Court offices or the court registrars to let them know what cases are proceeding and when they are likely to proceed.

3. REPORTING COURTS AND SIMILAR BODIES

It might be thought that the question of what could and could not be reported would be a simple one dealt with in a single statute with a comprehensive schedule. This is not so: it involves the consideration of common law, constitutional and statutory matters, some of which (notably in relation to the reporting of Oireachtas committees) are not free from doubt.

Statutory and constitutional provisions tend to relate to specific cases. It is extremely important to construe statutory provisions in particular with a common law background in mind: just because there is no statutory provision for the reporting of a particular type of proceeding, or for privilege for such reports, does not mean that such privilege does not exist.

From a media point of view two questions arise in relation to any particular kind of hearing or proceeding:

(a) Can it be reported?

(b) Is the report privileged?

Common Law

In the words of a leading textbook "the law recognises that the public has an interest in receiving fair and accurate reports in certain proceedings, such as those in courts and parliament, notwithstanding that the proceedings may contain statements defamatory of individuals". It is important to note that the courts and parliament were mentioned merely by way of example: other public bodies are also covered such as a tribunal of enquiry. Moreover, this privilege is supplemental to any privilege conferred by statute and not replaced by it.

Privilege in common law will normally be qualified privilege only and accordingly can be lost, *e.g.* by proof of malice.

While statutory privilege often confines the class of person who may publish such reports, *e.g.* newspapers or broadcasters, common law privilege applies to everyone and therefore covers non-newspaper, periodical publications or pamphlets and books.

Court Reporting: Common Law

Reports of court proceedings at common law

This privilege extends to judicial proceedings of any kind before a properly constituted court opened to the public. It applies to courts at every level, coroners courts, public sittings relating to bankruptcy and preliminary or interlocutory hearings.

In each case, however, this common-law privilege is open to regulation by statute, subject to the constitutional provisions considered below. It is not entirely clear to what extent common-law privilege applies to proceedings before foreign courts but the huge probability is that it applies at least to proceedings which may be supposed to have an interest for the public or some section of it in this country. No privilege attaches to the report of proceedings lawfully held in camera.

Common-law privilege will also attach to reports of the hearings of quasi-judicial tribunals considering matters in which the public have an interest, *e.g.* the beef tribunal.

To qualify for common-law privilege, the report of such proceedings must be fair and accurate, though not necessarily verbatim. A summary is perfectly acceptable so long as it is a fair summary. If proceedings last over a number of days the media is entitled to report them as they occur. However, it is not acceptable to carry an accurate report of the plaintiff's or prosecution's case and to fail to reflect the defendant's attack on it either by cross examination or otherwise at all. Some years ago the media in reporting a criminal case gave considerable prominence to prosecuting counsel's opening speech and then failed to report the evidence for either side or the fact that two days later the defendant was acquitted. Such a report is not of course "fair and accurate".

However, if a report is generally fair and accurate a slight inaccuracy will not deprive it from privilege although a significant inaccuracy will have that effect.

The report must be confined to what transpired in court including documents read or exhibited therein. If there is an issue as to the admissibility of certain evidence or documents it is unwise to report their contents until this issue has been determined.

Common-law privilege does not extend to reporting a matter which is blasphemous, indecent or seditious or (of course) contrary to statute. It should be noted that section 14 of the Censorship of Publications Act 1929 provides:

> "(1) It shall not be lawful to print or publish or cause or procure to be printed or published in relation to any judicial proceedings —
>
> > (a) any indecent matter the publication of which would be calculated to injure public morals or
> > (b) any indecent medical surgical or physiological details the publication of which would be calculated to injure public morals".

Apart from the criminal penalties for breach of such and prohibition, such material will not be protected by privilege of common law.

Court Reporting under the Constitution and Statute Law

Article 34.1 of the Constitution provides that:

> "Justice shall be administered in courts established by law . . . and save in such special and limited cases as may be prescribed by law shall be administered in public."

The effect of this provision is that the open administration of justice is to be the norm: exceptions must be prescribed by law (as opposed, for instance, to the discretion of the judge) and what transpires in public may of course be reported to the public. This puts beyond doubt the existence of the common law qualified privilege in relation to such matters.

Furthermore, section 18 of the Defamation Act 1961 confers a privilege, which appears to be absolute on fair and accurate reports, published contemporaneously, of court proceedings held in public. The "fair and accurate" requirement is identical to that considered above in relation to common-law privilege. The requirement of contemporaneity would cover reports in the next edition of a newspaper or similar publication after the report, but not a book or film made a considerable time later: such a publication may be able to avail of common-law privilege.

Note that this privilege, like its common law equivalent, relates to court proceedings held "in public". There is now variety of unconnected statutory provisions providing for hearings "in camera", "otherwise than in public" or "in chambers". There are other provisions affecting the type of material which can be published, *e.g.* prohibiting material identifying certain persons.

Provisions for hearing otherwise than in public

Section 45(1) of the Courts (Supplemental Provisions) Act 1961 provides:

> "Justice may be administered otherwise than in public in any of the following cases:
>
> (a) applications of an urgent nature for relief by way of habeus corpus, bail, prohibition or injunctions.
> (b) matrimonial causes and matters.
> (c) lunacy and minor matters.
> (d) proceedings involving the disclosure of a secret manufacturing process."

These, of course, are in addition to other cases prescribed by law.

In relation to "applications of an urgent nature" for reliefs of the kind mentioned, the rationale for this exception to the constitutional requirement of open justice is purely a practical one. A person seeking very urgent relief such as habeas corpus (an order to vindicate his right to liberty) or certain kinds of injunction, may not be able to wait for a scheduled sitting of the court. He may have to apply late at night or over a weekend wherever a judge can be found. For example, a person may seek habeas corpus because he is threatened with deportation within the next few hours, or may seek an injunction against a newspaper about something which is due to be published in the following day's edition. Applications of this kind are often heard in a judge's home or other convenient place. It may be impractical in certain circumstances to hear them publicly.

Moreover, applications of this kind never determine the entire issue between the parties. In the case of habeas corpus the most that can be obtained is a "conditional order" and in the case of an injunction, an interim order. In each case, there will be a full hearing shortly afterwards with the other side on notice and before a court sitting in the ordinary way.

It is now established that the rationale behind this exception is the urgency and not the nature of the relief itself. In the well-known case of *Agricultural Credit Corporation v. Irish Business*,[1] application for an interim injunction was made at a judge's home on the basis, amongst other things, that the article in question relied on leaked documents in relation to which the plaintiff was entitled to confidentiality and the protection of its copyright. The High Court granted an interim order. The plaintiff then gave notice of the order to a variety of media interests stating that the hearing by order of the judge had been held in camera and that the fact that the order had been made could not be published. It is not clear how much support this contention had in the order itself. However, when the case came up for interlocutory hearing an application to hear the case in camera was refused on the basis that the hearing was, unlike the interim hearing, not an urgent one and accordingly section 45(1)(a) could not apply.

On the basis of this, decisions can be confidentially stated as there is no suggestion whatever that the mere fact that the application for relief is for an injunction on one of the other reliefs specified does not justify a hearing otherwise than in public. Moreover, the reference to urgency must be interpreted as a reference to a degree of urgency so great that a normal sitting of the court cannot be awaited and not merely to the fact that there is a degree of urgency attaching to the application.

Matrimonial Causes and Matters

By virtue of a variety of statutes, this general reference in section 45 has been applied to virtually every kind of family proceedings. What varying forms of words, it applies to separations, divorces, maintenance applications, Family Home Protection Act applications, applications for protection and barring orders, applications under the Married Women's Status Act 1957 (if either party requested it) and applications under the Marriages Act 1972, the Adoption Acts and, at least where a party requested, two applications for declarations of paternity.

---

[1] *Irish Times*, August 9, September 10, 1985.

The rationale for this restriction is so that family matters can be determined in what former Chief Justice O'Higgins described, in the context of a guardianship case, as "a decent privacy". This is absolutely essential because countless persons would be deterred from instituting or defending proceedings of a very intimate nature if they were liable to be reported. In *Re Kennedy & McCann*,[3] it was stated in the strongest terms that any publication which interferes with this privacy will be regarded as a serious contempt of court even where (as in that case) one of the parties had positively sought such publicity.

However, if matrimonial proceedings are associated with other proceedings (an application for a non-matrimonial injunction; an attack on the Constitutionality of a statute) the protection will be strictly limited to the part of the proceedings which can be described as a matrimonial cause or matter. In such circumstances, however, the judge may request that the identities of parties or other details would not be revealed.

Lunacy and Minor Matters

As far as minors are concerned, there is a considerable degree of overlap with the matrimonial jurisdiction. The prohibition here applies to applications for the maintenance of children, matrimonial or otherwise, guardianship matters, applications under the Child Care Acts and certain proceedings under the Succession Act. Where a child is a defendant in a criminal proceeding the media are entitled to be present but the anonymity of the minor must be preserved by not naming him or publishing other identifying material.

Proceedings Involving the Disclosure of a Secret Manufacturing Process

This might relate to certain applications involving the use of patented processes and similar matters. Again, the rationale is the fear that persons would be put off reporting to the courts at all if a secret process in which, perhaps, they had invested a great deal of time or large amounts of money, had to be publicly revealed.

---

2 *Kennedy & McCann, In Re* [1976] I.R. 382.

Criminal Cases

A very wide range of provisions apply to different acts of criminal proceedings. In particular, the fact that criminal cases of a sexual nature should be a warning to a journalist to investigate his or her right to report.

Preliminary examination All indictable criminal cases are first the subject of a preliminary examination in the District Court, unless this is waived by the defendant. This consists of the service of certain documents and statements on the defendant, the hearing of submissions (if any) by either party and the examination of witnesses "on deposition" by either party, followed by the consideration of the material by the District Judge and a decision by him to send the accused forward for trial, or to refuse to do so. These preliminary proceedings are governed by the Criminal Procedure Act 1967 and they are held in open court except "where the court is satisfied because of the nature or circumstances or the case or otherwise in the interests of Justice" to the public should be excluded. Even when this occurs, however, the press are not to be excluded but there are significant limitations on what can be published.

Section 17(2) of the Criminal Procedure Act 1967 provides:

> "No person should publish or cause to be published any information as to any particular preliminary examination other than a statement of fact that such examination in relation to a named person on a specified charge has been held, and of the decision thereon".

This is in the interest of preserving the accused's right to a fair trial. In the nature of the preliminary examination the whole or at least the great bulk of the evidence is likely to be prosecution evidence, usually with no facility for cross-examination or other testing. There is, however provision for the accused to ask the judge to permit publication of what goes on at the preliminary examination. An accused may wish this to happen, for example, because he thinks it may cause witnesses to come forward. The Act relates to all cases which are the subject of preliminary examinations.

Sexual Offences The usual rule in relation to sexual offences now is that the public are excluded from such hearings, at least while the complainant is giving evidence. Bona fide representatives of the press are, however, permitted to remain. Any known material likely to lead members of the public to identify the victim or, unless there is a conviction, the defendant, cannot be published. After conviction, it may still be impossible to identify the defendant if to do so would tend to lead to the identification of the victim.

Miscellaneous provisions for hearing otherwise than in public Appeals to the Circuit Court from the Income Tax Appeal Commissioners are held in camera but cases stated to the High Court (that is, requests for guidance by the Commissioners or a Circuit Court judge raising specified points of law) are heard in public.

Applications under section 205 of the Companies Act 1963 (oppression of minorities) may be heard in camera "if in the opinion of the court the hearing or proceedings under this section would involve the disclosure of information, publication of which would be seriously prejudicial to the legitimate interests of the company".

The Companies (Amendment) Act 1990, which, *inter alia*, provides for the appointment of an examiner to a company and that an application for such an appointment may be made "otherwise than in public" if the court considers that the interests of the company or of the creditors as a whole so require.

4. DEFAMATION

STRIKING A BALANCE

The Constitution protects both the right to one's "good name" and the right to freedom of expression. Neither right is absolute, each qualifies the other. If the right to good name were absolute, no criticism or statements of a damaging kind would be possible. If the right to freedom of expression were absolute, a citizen's reputation would be unprotected even against lies. Accordingly the law seeks to strike a balance. It does this through the law of defamation.

CONCEPTS AND TERMINOLOGY

The key principles of the media law of defamation are these: a person has a right not to have his reputation damaged by a false statement which discredits him. But a journalist (or anyone else) has an absolute right to publish anything which can be shown to be true or substantially true. Moreover, in relation to matters of public interest there is broad scope for fair comment on facts truly stated. In some circumstances there may be a right to publish a statement which turns out to be false, by reason of privilege.

The whole law of defamation is about the application of these principles to the myriad of individual cases which occur. In doing so, the law has evolved over many years certain rules and definitions.

Remedies

Nearly all these rules and definitions have developed in the context of the main remedy by which the law provides for an attack on one's reputation: the civil action for damages. In rare and extreme circumstances, a defamation may be a criminal offence: this is dealt with separately below. Furthermore the court has a power to prevent the publication of a defamation by injunction. The conditions for obtaining this relief are so restrictive that a plaintiff will rarely be able to meet them.

Method

The simplest way to approach the central concepts and definitions is to consider first the essential elements of a stateable action for defamation, and secondly the available defences. A word of warning: some of the key words seem familiar but in this context they have a meaning vitally different from that found in ordinary usage. This is particularly true of the first and basic term, publication.

Publication

In the law of defamation, publication means any communication to a third party, *i.e.* to a person other than the speaker or writer on the one hand and the person spoken about on the other. You can say what you like about me to my face, or in a private letter: there is no publication in law until a third party hears or reads it. The person who communicates material is called the publisher. This term is used whether the communication takes the form of a private conversation, a newspaper article or a television broadcast.

Words

All material communicated to a third party whether orally or by the written word, or by drawing, cartoon, diagram, gesture or broadcast, are legally described as "words".[1]

Libel and Slander

Words communicated by speaking only, if defamatory, are slander. Words communicated in writing or other permanent form, if defamatory, are libel. Section 15 of the Broadcasting Act 1961 provides that broadcast defamations are libel, not slander.

The significance of the distinction is that slander is generally actionable only as proof of "special" (*i.e.* specific and provable) damage. In the case of the libel, once publication is proved, the law presumes that damage has been suffered. The plaintiff can lead evidence to "aggravate" or maximise the damage and the defendant to "mitigate" or minimise it, but some damage is presumed.

---

[1] *Gatley on Libel and Slander* (8th ed., 1981), para. 3.

Who is a "publisher"?

Media law is naturally concerned in the main with libel rather than slander. But the distinction is not always an easy one. Consider two examples.

(a) A man speaking confidentially to his wife in a restaurant is overheard to say something untrue and very damaging about a prominent personality. The eavesdropper tells a friend who tells a journalist who writes it up for publication. A newspaper prints it, and distributes it. Here, the first speaker has "published" the story to his wife.

This publication is slander only and is in any event probably privileged as a communication between husband and wife are deemed to be privileged.

The eavesdropper's publication to his friend is slander only. If he is sued and has no defence, he is responsible only for the publication made by him to the one person he spoke to.

The friend's publication to the journalist may be slander only, or may be libel. Which it is depends on whether the friend knew the person in question was a journalist who would publish the tale. If he did, the friend will be remanded as participating in the publication of the subsequent printed story – a libel.

The journalist's publication of the written story is clearly a libel, as is the newspaper's publication by printing and distribution. The journalist is jointly responsible ("liable") with the newspaper for the news distribution, because he clearly and willingly helped to bring it about. In legal terms he is a "concurrent wrongdoer", as is the printer.

Technically, each separate sale of the paper is a fresh publication to each purchaser, for which each vendor is separately liable. Distributors and newsagents have, however, a special statutory defence.[2]

The liability of each separate publisher can be an important consideration, especially if the financial standing of the newspaper is doubtful. Printers and distributors may seek to protect their position by seeking "indemnities" from newspaper proprietors. Journalists' liabilities in practice are covered by their employer.

---

[2] See below, *Distributor's Defence* in Chapter 7 below.

(b) A public figure gives an "on the record" interview to a journalist, who tapes it in his presence. The paper prints the interview including material defamatory of a third party. After the interview is over the journalist leaves the tape on during a private conversation in which the public figure attacks the motivation of a third party who has bad mouthed him to the journalist. This, too, is printed.

In this instance the public figure is jointly liable with the newspaper and journalist for any libel in the "on the record" interview. This is because he intended what he said to be printed and said it for that purpose. He is a publisher of the written interview as well as the spoken words.

The same cannot be said of the private conversation and any defamation in this is slander only. More significantly, the public figure may have a defence to a slander action if he is replying to an attack made on him to the paper he is addressing. This is an aspect of privilege.[3] But this defence may extend only to the private response to a private attack, not to the further publication of it to all the paper's readers. Since the public figure did not consciously participate in the latter publication, he is not liable for it.

These examples illustrate the important point that a single publication in the media may be the result of one or more previous private, semi-public or public statements to the same effect. Each such statement is a separate "publication" and different legal considerations may apply to each.

It also follows that the plaintiff may sue any one or more, or all, of the "publishers". Sometimes, as in *Quirke & O'Regan v. C.R.H.* or *Allied Discount Cards Ltd v. Bord Fáilte*,[4] the plaintiff will not sue the media organ involved (R.T.É. and The *Irish Press* respectively) but will proceed directly against the originator of the libel. In such cases the journalist who conducted the interview may be required to identify the person who spoke to him. This course will, however, usually be followed only in circumstances where the originator is a good "mark" for damages. Usually the media organ is the easiest mark.

---

[3] See under "Defences" below).
[4] [1991] 2 I.R. 185.

There is another, little considered, consequence of the legal definition of "publisher". The Civil Liability 1964 provides that all persons who participate in the commission of a tort or civil wrong are "concurrent wrong doers". All are liable to be sued. If one is sued and the other(s) are not, the defendant can seek to join the other wrongdoers and seek "contribution or indemnity" from them. This means they can be made responsible for some or all of the damages and costs.

There is no legal reason why media defendants do not seek to use these provisions against those who misinform them. No doubt they feel that doing so would kill off sources of information or quotation. But this remedy is available, and should be considered more often, especially in the case of larger public or private bodies who court the media and seek to use it for their ends.

Is it defamatory?

Once the plaintiff has established the publication he is aggrieved about, and has identified the publisher(s) of it, he must show that it is "defamatory" of him. The "onus", *i.e.*, the legal obligation to demonstrate, is on the plaintiff.

There is no litmus test to determine what is defamatory and what is not. In general, however, a defamatory statement is one which:

(a) is false;

(b) tends to discredit a person by damaging his good name, *i.e.* the regard in which he is held, his reputation or character;

(c) does so in the eyes of reasonable, right-thinking people.

Each of these aspects requires further examination.

(a) *Falsity*

Only a false statement is actionable. Any true statement, however unfair, hurtful or intrusive, can be published with impunity as a defence of justification is available to the publisher. Furthermore, this defence may be available even though part of what is published is false. But the onus is on the defendant to prove the truth of what he publishes.[5]

(b) *Discrediting in character or reputation*

Not every statement that is false and damaging is defamatory. To be defamatory a statement must be false and such as makes people think the worse of the plaintiff in a moral or social sense.

For example, to say, falsely, that a professional person has retired from practice due to ill-health may well cause damage but is not actionable as defamation. This is because ill-health is a misfortune not normally causing a loss of social or moral standing in the eyes of reasonable people.

However, to say that a professional person has ceased to practice after being "struck off" for misconduct is clearly defamatory if untrue.

At a trial in the High Court, it is for the judge to rule on whether the words complained of are *capable* of a defamatory meaning, and for the jury to say if they are, in fact, defamatory of the plaintiff.

Decisions as to what is and is not defamatory will vary over time and with circumstances, including especially the identity of the plaintiff. Thus, at one time it was defamatory of a person to say that he was a Roman Catholic, or a Francophile or, later, pro-German, but it is obvious that none of these are now defamatory in themselves.

On the other hand, it is now gravely defamatory to say of a person that he is a member, or associate, of the I.R.A.[6] but this would not have been so in Ireland in 1922.

A statement which is not obviously defamatory may defame a particular plaintiff due to his special circumstances. For example, to say that a person has got married is not usually defamatory but could defame a person who is a practising Catholic priest because it suggests hypocrisy, breach of church rules and an irregular position in his profession.

Although there is no single formula for identifying a defamatory statement, experience suggests that certain types of statement are almost always defamatory. These include:

(a) Statements that a person has committed a crime. Except in the most trivial cases, these will be found to be defamatory. Allegations of very serious crimes, *e.g.* murder, subversive activities or drug dealing will attract very substantial damages. This may seem obvious, but quite a number of such allegations have been

---

[5] See "Defences" below.
[6] *McDonagh v. News Group Newspapers*, Irish Times Law Reports, December 27, 1993.

published in Ireland over the last decade. False allegations of offences that are minor (in the legal sense) may be seriously defamatory. A false allegation of drunk driving caused *Hibernia* magazine to go out of business in the 70s, and would probably be even more seriously regarded today.

(b) An allegation reflecting on a person's behaviour or capacity in his profession or trade. If this kind of allegation is seriously damaging it can attract large damages. Allegations of professional or commercial dishonesty (whether amounting to a crime or not) are extremely risky.

(c) Allegations of sexual immorality, especially if they involve suggestions of adultery, family irresponsibility or hypocrisy. Such allegations are well established as defamatory.

It has yet to be established whether it is defamatory in contemporary Ireland to state merely that a person is having a non-marital sexual relationship. The Slander of Women Act 1891 makes a *slander*, alleging "unchastity" of a woman actionable without proof of special damage.[7] Whether an allegation of a specific non-marital relationship is an allegation of "unchastity" has yet to be determined. The practice for such cases has been to settle unless there is a defence of justification available.

This subject matter has increased in practical importance with the rise of the gossip column. Such allegations are often based on third hand information which is impossible to establish in evidence. Informants of these topics are notoriously elusive if asked to give evidence.

The decriminalisation of homosexuality does not necessarily mean that a false allegation of homosexuality made against a person is not defamatory. The *Jason Donovan* case suggests that this allegation is still defamatory, even in England. Such an allegation against a married person, a parent or a person of ostensibly heterosexual habits is almost certainly defamatory.

Allegations of consorting, with prostitutes are defamatory.[8]

Allegations of sexual activities which amount to crimes (*e.g.* rape,

---

[7] See now s.16 of the Defamation Act 1961.

[8] *Andrews v. Irish Press*, unreported, High Court, 1987.

child abuse, intercourse with an underage person) are clearly defamatory.

In *Quigley v. Creation Ltd*[9] it was suggested that a false statement
about a woman to the effect that she had been the *victim* of a rape
(or, presumably, any sexual offence), might be defamatory as "ex-
posing her to undesirable interest".

(d) Allegations of misconduct by public officials are likely to be
    defamatory. A Dáil answer to a question by Deputy Mary Harney
    in 1989 revealed details of a practice whereby officials may be
    financially supported by the State in the bringing of such actions.

(e) Allegations of insolvency against an individual or company and
    statements casting doubt on one's ability to pay one's debts as
    they fall due. The consequences of such allegations can be very
    serious.

Allegations of commercial or professional "sharp practice", not
amounting to crime, can be defamatory. Such stories have this in
common with sexual ones: informants are often eager to see a story
published but are most elusive and unwilling to give evidence later.

Examples The following are examples of allegations in the main-
stream media which have come to the attention of Irish lawyers in
recent years:
- that the plaintiff is a mass murderer;
- that the plaintiff is a manufacturer of bombs;
- that the plaintiff is engaged in a campaign of terrorism including
  the murder of innocent civilians;
- that the plaintiff has bribed public officials;
- that the plaintiff is a drug dealer;
- that the plaintiff and his family suffer from AIDS;
- that the plaintiff is a prostitute or a procuress;
- that the plaintiff is unfaithful to his or her spouse;
- that the plaintiff is insolvent;
- that the plaintiff's business is a front for criminals;

---

[9] [1971] I.R. 269.

– that the plaintiff's incompetence as a professional person has needlessly caused deaths;
– that the plaintiff has deceived his clients and cheated them out of money;
– that the plaintiff is incompetent in his profession;
– that the plaintiff has defrauded a state scheme;
– that the plaintiff, a married man, is actively homosexual;
– that the plaintiff is a spy;
– that the plaintiff is a petty tyrant at his work.

Most of these cases settled. In all those that fought, the plaintiff succeeded. Some of the most dramatic were in English papers circulating here.

Libels about journalists

Journalists and media executives normally see themselves as potential defendants rather than plaintiffs. But, surprisingly often, the boot is on the other foot. A statement that a journalist is a "libellous journalist" is defamatory as also are any words to the same effect. In the 1950s the well-known writer, Honor Tracey, successfully sued the *Daily Telegraph* for a retraction and apology it had published in relation to an article written by her on this basis.[10] In Ireland, Aengus Fanning, editor of *The Sunday Independent* and John Mulcahy (*Hibernia* and *The Phoenix*), have both been successful libel plaintiffs.

The standards of reasonable, right-thinking-people

It is not enough to show that some small, quirky group of the community think the worse of the plaintiff. The court will consider whether he has been damaged in the eyes of reasonable, right thinking persons, or some significant group of them, large or small.

To say that one member of a criminal gang "peached" on the others may lower him in the view of criminals and associates. But their standards are not ones the court can approve or apply, so there is no action. To say that a person is a practising Catholic may cause

---

[10] *Tracey v. Kennsley Newspapers Ltd*, *The Times*, April 9, 1954.

fanatical fundamentalists or rationalists to think the worse of him, but for the same reason, is not actionable.

In *Berry v. Irish Times*[11] the paper printed a photograph of a protestor's placard on which the plaintiff, a former Secretary of the Department of Justice, was called a "felon setter". This, literally, means one who attempts to bring criminals to justice. Both the jury and the Supreme Court on appeal declined to find the words defamatory. The Supreme Court found that though the words might injure the plaintiff in the minds of some people, their standards were not those of reasonable or right thinking members of the community.

The court, then, will not approve the standards of people with anti-social or utterly irrational views. But it will acknowledge that, short of this, individuals and groups are entitled to strong views even if they are not widely shared.

Especially if the plaintiff is himself a member of such a group, their standards may be important. Thus, for example, the views and standards of strictly observant Jews, though a tiny minority of the population, are both reasonable and capable of being held by persons who are "right thinking". They may be highly relevant if, for example, the plaintiff is a Rabbi.

Interpreting the words complained of

We have been considering, in general terms, the meaning of defamation. We now move from the general to the particular, and ask: how does the court determine whether or not any particular publication conveys a defamatory meaning? And, if it is defamatory, what precise meaning or meanings does it convey?

Ordinary and natural meanings

Often, there is no difficulty. A statement that "Smith is the biggest heroin dealer in Dublin" has a plain meaning which is plainly defamatory. Lawyers say it is defamatory "in its natural and ordinary meaning".

These words, in their ordinary sense (which includes inferences which a reasonable person would draw) mean:

---

[11] [1973] I.R. 365.

Defamation

- Smith deals in heroin;
- he does so on a bigger scale than anyone else in Dublin;
- he is a criminal;
- he is engaged in anti-social activity of a gross kind;
- he does so for financial profit.

Innuendo

Suppose that, though not stated in the publication, some but not all the readers know some additional facts about Smith, *viz.*, he is a teacher, a county councillor and a prominent anti-drugs campaigner.

To those who know these facts, the words have additional meanings. These include:

- Smith is a hypocrite;
- he is unfit to practice his profession;
- he has deceived those who voted for him;
- he is unworthy to be an elected representative.

Because these meanings are not apparent unless one has information not contained in the publication, they are "innuendoes".

Sometimes, a statement is not defamatory at all without an innuendo. Thus: "Smith goes twice a week to No. 20 Main Street" will mean nothing to many people, But to those who know that there is a brothel at that address it is clearly defamatory.

Similarly, "Mr Smith, solicitor, paid promptly for his swimming pool with a cheque drawn on his client account". To solicitors, accountants and many others, but not to the general public, this will mean that Smith has appropriated his clients' money. This is because they know that a solicitor is not entitled to use his client's money in the client account for personal expenditure. This additional information gives rise to an "innuendo".

Knowledge

A journalist may, of course, write a passage which is defamatory by innuendo without himself knowing the facts which render it defamatory. This does not alter the defamation, because "defamation is a question of fact, not of intention". But it may be relevant to the question of damages. In a defamation action, the plaintiff's lawyers will include in their written "Statement of Claim" all the defamatory meanings they claim the publication bears. The defendant may admit all, deny all or admit some and deny others.

If no innuendo is pleaded, *i.e.* specifically mentioned in the Statement of Claim, the plaintiff will be confined to the "natural and ordinary meaning" of the words. No evidence will be allowed as to what the words mean because the court or jury is deemed to know the natural and ordinary meaning of words.

If an innuendo is pleaded, the plaintiff can call evidence to prove the "extrinsic facts", *i.e.* facts not contained in the publication which give rise to the innuendo meaning.

Thus, in the example about the solicitor, above, he would call experts to establish the meaning of the words, "client account", the rules about such accounts and the fact that knowledge of these matters was widespread in certain circles.

Sometimes the extrinsic facts relied on relate to the words used themselves. A technical word, a slang word, a word in a foreign language, may all require evidence to prove their real meaning.

Thus, a phrase like "Ugandan discussions" as used in *Private Eye* has come to mean sexual activities, even to many people who don't know how the term originated. An English court was satisfied that the term "fruit flavoured" as applied to the pianist Liberace meant "homosexual". In each instance there is an innuendo based on extrinsic facts, *viz.* the extended meanings these terms have taken on over a period of years.

Sometimes a word will have a very different connotation in a particular area and/or in a particular generation to that which it originally bore. Thus, the word "felon setter" is probably not part of ordinary "English" today. When it was, it meant a person who tried to bring criminals to justice.

In *Berry v. Irish Times*[12] above, the plaintiff complained of the description "20th Century Felon Setter" In Irish use, he felt, it meant an informer, a traitor, a sneak, one who betrayed his own people to a brutal alien power. But he did not plead an innuendo. Accordingly, both the jury in the High Court and the Supreme Court in the subsequent appeal interpreted the words literally and found no defamation.

---

[12] See note 11.

Some common problems of interpretation

Let us now look at the "heroin dealer" example in various different forms.

Suppose it read: "Jones says: Smith deals in heroin" or "Jones lashes 'heroin dealer' Smith".

These forms seek to distance the publishers from the allegation by attributing it to Jones. As a means of avoiding liability this doesn't work. If it did, anything could be published as long as someone, somewhere was prepared to say it. It is of course true that Jones said what is reported, but if the media repeat what he says, with or without attribution, they made his statement their own. This is an important rule of general application: A defamation is no less a defamation because it is reported in indirect speech, or in the passive voice (". . . is believed to . . ."), whether or not the original source is mentioned.

The only exception to this is where the original remark was made in public in circumstances of *absolute* privilege (in the Dáil or Courts or equivalent circumstances).[13]

It is important to note that a report of what Jones said may be actionable even though Jones said it in circumstances of *qualified* privilege.[14] Thus, for example, if Jones is the headmaster of the school where Smith works, he will be entitled to tell the Board of Management, privately, what he believes about Smith. But if a newspaper reports what he said to the public, the only defence is that the statement is true.

Now consider: "Smith suspected of heroin dealing" or "Heroin deals: police suspect Smith".

These are not statements in indirect speech that Smith is a heroin dealer. They are statements that some people (identified as the police in the second example) suspect him of heroin dealing. The plaintiff's lawyers would argue that in each case (and certainly the second) the natural implication is that there are grounds for suspicion which has caused people who know the facts to suspect him. This is defamatory in itself because it tends to make "reasonable right thinking" people suspicious of him. Would you employ or vote for someone whom the police reasonably suspect of drug dealing?

---

[13] See "Defences" below.
[14] See "Defences" below.

The same effect is created by a statement like: "Police sources were yesterday naming Smith as the subject of their investigations in the heroin dealing-case".

Assuming-that the police were indeed doing-this "off the record", that fact is no defence of any headline worded in the way mentioned above. More fundamentally, if Smith sues it will be necessary for the defendant to prove that police sources were naming Smith, and told the journalist so. But the policeman perhaps shouldn't have been talking to the reporter in the first place and won't give evidence or allow the journalist to name him. The plaintiff may then suggest that the whole story is malicious invention and this may be difficult to contradict. No short-cuts based on attributing defamatory sentiments to others will work. If the "Smith" story is to be written at all, it will have to be on the basis of finding-out the facts which led to the suspicions and printing those facts, if they stand up.

Very odd meanings   In 1993 a pop star called D. sued a magazine for alleging that he was homosexual. He won, and recovered large damages.

For several weeks after this the programme "Have I Got News for You" referred to D. at every opportunity. In particular, it said over and over 'D' is certainly not homosexual. What did this mean? The tone, expressions and repetition all suggested it meant exactly the opposite of what it ostensibly stated. Whether it does or not would he decided by a jury, if D. sued again. Especially in the case of broadcast material, words can convey the opposite of what they state on paper. Or, they may make a strong negative statement which nonetheless conveys a positive.

Consider: "Friends and, political associates strongly denounced suggestions that Mr Smith was involved in heroin dealing".

This may be a perfectly fair report, for example if the "suggestions" have already received wide publicity. But if no such suggestions have been made publicly so that this is the first the readers knew of them, a court or jury may well view the publication as constituting a statement that Smith was, or was suspected of being, involved in heroin dealing. This view may be particularly attractive if the media cannot or will not identify the source of the "suggestions".

Every school child learns at an early stage that a phrase like "That's really great", can convey anything from genuine delight to "you've really screwed up" to "We're in trouble now", and "It couldn't be worse". Not surprisingly, the law also takes account of the great variety of meanings possible for words and phrases, especially where ambiguity is deliberately sought (as by whoever arranged that "tired and emotional" should mean "drunk").

There is no easy formula for the interpretation of oblique phrases, but one usually knows exactly what is conveyed. Some years ago an Irish publication said that a prominent person. in his youth, had been given roses by Rock Hudson. The written defence denied any defamatory suggestion, but the case was settled on the morning of the hearing. There can be little doubt what view the jury would have taken.

Identification

When words are proved to be defamatory, and to have been published in the media, there is still another test to be met before the plaintiff can rest his case. He must show that they are published "of and concerning" *him* – not someone else, or a vague group of people, or a notional person, but himself.

Two main points arise:

1. The plaintiff must be named or otherwise identified so as to convey to reasonable readers, or some section of them, that the publication is about him.

2. If it is conveyed in any way that the publication relates to the plaintiff then it is irrelevant to the question of libel that the defendant did not intend to refer to the plaintiff. But the defence has other options.[15]

The most common form of identification is by name, and here there will usually be no problem for the plaintiff. But identification can take place in other ways as well. In one case[16] a newspaper carried a front page report of a notorious criminal case, which contained serious allegation against the defendant. Beside this, it carried a photograph of a completely uninvolved person, claiming he was the defendant leaving court. The subject of the photograph sued, claiming he was identified as the defendant. The paper settled.

---

[15] See "Defences" below.
[16] *O'Kelly v. Irish Press Newspapers, Irish Times*, May 23-28, 1992.

Again, a photograph of the plaintiff in the centre of the article which describes abuses, but does not name him, may be seen as linking him to the text, especially if no explanation is forthcoming.[17]

Identification by Inference

Quite often, a publication will fail to identify anyone to the average reader, but will give enough information to allow people with special knowledge to identify the plaintiff or to make enquiries which leads to his identification.

Thus, to say "If competent medical care had been available Mr Smith would not have died", is defamatory of Smith's doctor to those who knew Smith was under his care in the period prior to his death.

The principle is: do the words contain enough information to allow some reasonable person, with or without special knowledge, to identify the plaintiff as the subject of the article?

If they do, it does not matter whether identification is by inference from the statements made, by inference from unstated facts known to the reader, or from initials, blanks, nicknames, or cryptic references, *e.g.* "The man from Mayo".

Individuals and Classes

While the law will recognise a reference to the, plaintiff, however oblique, it will not encourage over sensitive reactions to general statements. Thus, to say: "All journalists are liars" will not confer a right of action on any individual journalist. The class reference to "all journalists", is too broad to allow the identification by a reasonable person of any individual.

A statement may be actionable as containing an imputation, or as casting suspicion, on each member of it. In an old Irish case, a statement about "The clergy of Kingstown", of which there were 12, was held actionable by any one.

Similarly, a statement that some, or one, of a small class of people has done something discreditable, may defame each member. To say "either A or B is guilty" is plainly likely to damage each of them

---

[17] *Cooney v. Sunday World, Irish Times*, November 8, 1978.

and is actionable by either. As the class gets bigger, it is a question of fact for the jury to say whether, in all the circumstances, the individual plaintiff is identifiable by a *reasonable person.*

In practice identification will depend on the evidence available. If a number of witnesses who are apparently honest and rational give reasons why they personally identified the plaintiff, the defendant will need a strong case, including a convincing explanation as to who he was referring to, if he is to rebut the effect of such evidence.

Fictitious names

If a fictitious name is used in a news story, there is a risk that it will coincide with that of a real person. If in addition some details of the fictitious character also correspond, there is a real danger of identification of the real person as the subject of the story. Since the usual reason for the use of false names is the sensitive nature of the story, there is a clear risk of defamation.

This was illustrated in *Browne v. Independent Newspapers.*[18] A front page story spoke of complaints by builders of bribes they were forced to pay by corrupt planning officials. A box in this story referred readers to a "News Analysis" feature inside, about a builder who described what went on. This article, several thousand words long, began "Builder John Browne knew the score", and went on to say how he was forced to pay increasing bribes in brown paper bags which he could no longer afford to pay. He then went to the authorities, it was said.

The plaintiff was John Browne, builder. He – and he alone – was thus described in the Dublin phone book. Many respectable witnesses whose truthfulness was not challenged, swore that they believed the article referred to him. The paper pointed out that, at the very end of the article, thousands of words and several columns away from the references to Browne, there was a statement in italics that all names were fictitious. Most witnesses had simply not read that far and those who had thought it was a device inserted for legal reasons.

The judge (Carney J.) refused to hold with the paper's submission that a person who read part only of a long article was not a

---

[18] *Irish Times*, November 19, 1991.

"reasonable" person in law. He said it was for the jury to find whether the addendum, having regard to its contents and position, negatived the references to Browne.

The paper called no evidence whatever and therefore gave no explanation of why Browne's name was used, whether they had looked up the phone book, or who they were, in fact, referring to. The jury awarded Browne £75,000.

If a name is used in a piece of fiction the same principles apply. In such a case, however, more specific characteristics are revealed than in a news story. The coincidences, accidental or deliberate, with a real person, can be astonishing.[19]

CRIMINAL LIBEL

Historically, the publication of a serious libel has always been regarded as a crime as well as a civil wrong. Prosecutions for criminal libel in a non-media context still occasionally occur. An example is the sort of case where an identifiable person repeatedly paints grossly offensive statements about another in public places.

In a media context, however, criminal libel has become extremely rare. It was, indeed, on the point of becoming obsolete in the United Kingdom until the case of *Gleaves v. Deakin*,[20] and a series of cases initiated by Sir James Goldsmith against the publishers of *Private Eye*.

In Ireland, criminal libel is rarer still but it is undoubtedly still alive. That proposition was established in the case of *Hilliard v. Penfield Enterprises*.[21] In this case the relatives of a deceased gentleman were outraged by the publication of an alleged libel on him in the immediate aftermath of his death. Since libel is not one of the accepted cases of action, within the meaning of the Civil Liability Act, no civil action lies for a libel on a deceased person.

Section 8 of the Defamation Act 1961 provides that no criminal prosecution can be commenced against any proprietor, publisher, editor or other person responsible for the publication of a newspaper

---

[19] *Ross v. Hopkinson, The Times*, October 16, 17, 1956.
[20] [1980] A.C. 477
[21] [1990] 1 I.R. 138.

in respect of any libel without an order of the High Court after a hearing in camera. This protection does not extend to publications other than "newspapers" within the meaning of the Act.

In the *Hilliard* case, leave to prosecute for criminal libel was refused even though the judge was plainly sympathetic to the applicant, who was the deceased gentleman's widow. He went so far as to observe that it was difficult to believe that the individual defendants could "stoop so low" as to publish the libel complained of but he nevertheless refused leave to initiate a prosecution. Having regard to the view which which he formed on the libel itself, the case indicates, that the circumstances in which leave will be granted must be extremely aggravated.

In was formerly thought that criminal libel could be satisfied only when the libel was such as was calculated to lead to a breach of the peace, *i.e.* physical violence or threats thereof. The *Hilliard* case and the English authorities establish that this is not the sole characteristic of a criminal libel; but what is required is that the libel is truly serious and capable of "so greatly affecting a person's character and reputation so as to justify invoking criminal law and punishment instead of, or as well as, the civil law and damages" (*Gleaves v. Deakin*).[22]

In fact, a significant number of prosecutions or attempted prosecutions for criminal libel relate to the same circumstances as did *Hilliard*. The libel had been published of a deceased person and his relatives were determined to seek redress. The allegations have usually been of a particularly aggravated kind; in one English case it had been alleged that the applicant's deceased father, a contractor to the French army, had supplied meat taken from the bodies of dead French soldiers.

There has been a deal of academic discussion of reform of the law of libel by providing a remedy for a libel on a deceased person. If this were done, the case for retaining any offence at all might be re-examined.

Prior to *Hilliard*, the last previous application for permission to commence criminal libel prosecution was in 1975. There has been no case of alleged criminal libel in the media area since *Hilliard*.

---

[22] Note 20 above.

5. LIBEL : ASPECTS OF PROCEDURE AND TACTICS

Is There a Prima Facie Case?

The foregoing chapter provides a simple checklist to address the question – is there a *prima facie* case of libel or not? A *prima facie* case means simply a set of facts which, if uncontradicted by other evidence or challenged in their legal effect by technical argument, would entitle the plaintiff to judgment. If you swear you saw me break the window of your car and take out your radio, that is a *prima facie* case of larceny and malicious damage against me. I may be able to answer it in any number of ways, but unless I do I will be convicted.

Before an action for libel is intimated, the plaintiff's lawyers will have considered whether there is a *prima facie* case or not. But the mere fact that they have decided to proceed does not mean that there is in fact a *prima facie* case. The plaintiffs legal advice may be wrong, or (more likely) the lawyer may hope that the media defendant will be intimidated, or give in to save costs, even though there is no case, or only a doubtful one.

Preliminary letters

A claim may be initiated by letter, usually from a solicitor asserting that the plaintiff has been defamed and seeking some form of redress. Alternatively, legal proceedings may be started without correspondence by the issue of a "Plenary Summons", which is the originating document in a High Court defamation action.

A summons will very rarely issue without preliminary correspondence. Where this does happen, the plaintiff is signalling that the libel, in his view, is so serious and deliberate that there is no point in corresponding.

But in most cases, there will be correspondence. It is extremely important for a media defendant to read and assess the first letter properly and if appropriate to take steps to redress the wrong without delay. If that is not possible, preparations to fight are best made immediately.

First Question

A media defendant's first questions, once an action is intimated, are not technical ones. They are:

"Are we, as of today, quite happy with the publication? Are the facts true? How do we know? Does the solicitor's letter raise any issues of fact or meaning which we didn't consider before? Have we made any mistake?"

Mistake or Uneasy feeling

If you have made a mistake, or have an uneasy feeling, ask: Can this case be settled right away?

Except in the most serious cases and where for some reason either the plaintiff or the media defendant is determined to go to court, the first few days (sometimes hours) after publication is the best and cheapest time to settle.

This is because the plaintiff is just beginning to suffer damage. The calls and questions from family, friends and associates are just starting. The gossipy embellishments may not yet have begun. If he can secure, right away, an apology/clarification he may feel (correctly in many cases) that the trouble is nipped in the bud.

On the other hand, even a few days delay may change everything. He may have been "called in" by superiors or some formal or informal regulatory body. He may have seen a look of incredulity greet his explanations to friends and associates. To prevent further damage or to add force to his denials, he may have said "I'm suing, of course". Also, especially if the libel is of such a kind as causes hurt to spouses or children, the iron may enter his soul. Such a plaintiff feels that nothing that can happen later can be as bad as what he as already suffered, and determine to proceed.

Immediate action

If there is any feeling. of uneasiness at all, explore whether immediate settlement is available for a statement/apology and costs. In a serious case damages may be inevitable even at an early stage. Settlement now may cost one tenth or even less of the value (including both sides' costs) of the same case after a hearing.

Negotiation

Negotiations for a settlement are best undertaken by lawyers, for reasons to do with the complex operation of the "without prejudice" rule.[1] But if the plaintiff approaches the media himself, and you are fairly clear there has been an error and you want to settle, it may be worth negotiating to a conclusion there and then.

If you do this, remember that all that you say that isn't part of any offer to settle, is not protected from disclosure and may be proved in court. Thus it is very foolish to say "I have to admit we've been sloppy" or anything of that sort, unless, of course, it is obvious.

What the plaintiff wants

Sometimes it may transpire almost immediately that the parties are so far apart that no settlement is possible.

But even if this happens, assuming that all discussions have been kept without prejudice, no-one is any worse off for having tried.

If settlement is reached, the plaintiff will almost always want some printed statement. He may or may not insist on the word "apology". Sometimes a "statement" or "clarification" will do.

At a very early stage, plaintiffs are surprisingly undemanding about where and in what form a statement is published. This is because, at this stage, he is still focused on the people he knows personally to have read the libel, and he intends to show the retraction to them personally. Later – even a little later – he will begin to register emotionally that thousands of people whom he will never know also read it and will be much more demanding about prominence, print size, boxing and so on.

Equally, the contents of the statement will vary a good deal with the stage at which it is offered and the quality and experience of the plaintiff's legal advisers. A fairly bland statement, correcting some error and regretting any inconvenience could suffice. Many readers, however, will see this as just a bit of legalese, a mere hedge against litigation. A good lawyer, especially in a serious case, will

---

[1] See under "Defences" below.

require prominence, the use of the term "apology" and some explanation of how the defamation came to be printed (usually human error) and some reference to costs, damages or a contribution to charity. Any or all of these may be negotiable in a particular case and, sometimes, the client is so eager for an *immediate* statement that he will settle for less than his lawyers tell him should be available.

Costs

In a very early settlement a defendant will usually pay the plaintiff's costs on an "indemnity basis", *i.e.* the whole of his costs. A specific sum may be agreed or a formula like "reasonable costs on an indemnity basis" used. The amount will vary greatly with the gravity and complexity of the case.

Damages

In a debatable case, or one where the whole sting can be removed by apology, it may be possible to settle early without paying damages.

In a very bad case from the point of view of the media defendant, a huge saving, can still be made by making a realistic offer very early. Even the most aggrieved and best positioned plaintiff will usually be prepared to settle early at a relatively conservative valuation, and much less in costs, than would be the case after a hearing.

Assessment of the Case – and Balancing the Risks

All of the above is based on the assumption that, at first blush, the case is a doubtful one from the point of view of the media defendant – there's been a mistake or the story just won't stand up on examination. Surprisingly often, a newspaper and its advisers come to this conclusion, but two to three years after the publication, and on the eve of a court hearing. By that time both sides have incurred large costs and the settlement value of the case has greatly increased. Still worse, a lapse of time may have made impossible the investigation for a fighting defence which should have been undertaken years before.

When this happens, it is because the media defendant has put the case on the long finger. It has done a holding reply to the first letter, then passed the file to its solicitors. They too have temporised and the plaintiff has issued proceedings. These take on a life of their own which, mainly, the lawyers deal with. Then, after years of ignoring it, the journalist is asked to attend a pre-trial consultation because the case is listed in court.

This sorry tale repeats itself often. And for one good reason. About 50 per cent of libel actions just go away. From a defendant's point of view, the problem is trying to identify *which* 50 per cent is this particular case in?

Libel cases go away for many reasons. The person has a skeleton in the cupboard, which the media may know nothing about. He can't afford the risks. His life has changed and the case is history. He fears the media will take revenge. His family can't take the pressure. He's frightened of the costs. He can't face further publicity, and so on.

If a plaintiff's case goes dormant, it is rarely in the interests of the media defendant to revive it. But this policy of masterly inactivity, quite appropriate in 50 per cent of cases – is often applied by default to the other 50 per cent. This means that media defendants lose or settle more cases than they should, and pay large multiples of the minimum costs and damages by settling late instead of earlier where settlement is appropriate.

Therefore

- Review each case early, and often (*i.e.* every month to three months thereafter).

- If the decision is to defend, it should be a positive decision, not a default decision.

- If there's an obvious error or serious uneasiness try to settle right away – within days, even hours.

- In such a case, be prepared to be generous in the terms of a statement/apology, but avoid offering damages except in serious cases (multiple small settlements encourage claims).

- Remember: inadequacy of the offered statement/apology is the single most common reason for failures in early settlement talks. The differences rarely seem important in retrospect.

- If your first review, confirmed by legal advice, suggests that the case can and should be fought, start right away (see below).

- At all stages, make sure you know, not just what your lawyers think, but why. Put your view of the case, including a full statement of facts and evidence, in writing and get theirs in writing too. Focus meeting on the issues causing problems, determined in advance.

First review

At the first review:

- Divide the publication complained of into FACT and COMMENT.

- Is each statement of fact true or false? How do you know? Can you prove it? How?

- List the witnesses required. Get someone to get a statement from each.

- Be clear as to what each witness can and can't prove.

- Go through the article/story with the writer(s). Ascertain the source for each statement. Get and keep copies of all notes, drafts, proofs, tapes *etc.* See to preservation of originals.

- Approach all sources, whether usable as witnesses or not. Tell them of the case, to stop memories fading. See if they can find out more, if necessary. Make sure the writer keeps in touch with them. A turn in a case can make a peripheral witness central.

- List the comments in the article. List the facts on which they are based. Are these facts stated or indicated in the article? If merely indicated, where are they fully stated? Are they true? Perform the same exercise as for Statement of Fact.

- If the piece complained of consists of, or includes, statements by the plaintiff himself, whether to the writer of the piece or to someone else, get the notes of the interviewer of the occasion on which the statements were made. If possible, get the author of the notes to do a full statement on everything to do with the occasion in question.

Once these exercises have been done, the media defendant can address the question of which defence, or mix of defences, will be used.

6. DEFENCES TO LIBEL

There are some 13 defences which may in practice be available in a libel action. Frequently two or more of them can be used in combination. They vary considerably in their nature and effect. Some defences will exempt the defendant from liability altogether. Others will merely mitigate or reduce it. Some are strong positive defences while others merely consist of denying that the plaintiff has established the elements of a prima facie defence.

POSITIVE DEFENCES

1. Justification
2. Fair comment
3. Privilege
4. Consent

Justification

This is the most fundamental of all defences. It is a claim that the words complained of "are true in substance and in fact", to use the language of legal pleadings. The truth is a complete defence to an action for defamation. Once established, it protects the publication no matter how unfair, gratuitous, or intrusive it may be. Furthermore, if a publication contains two or more defamatory allegations against the plaintiff "the defence shall not fail by reason only that the truth of every charge is not proved, if the words not proved to be true do not materially injure the plaintiff's reputation having regard to the truth of the remaining charges".[1] Furthermore a plea of justification will not fail because of minor inaccuracies in detail so long as the gist or substance of the story is correct. Thus, an allegation that a person who has been convicted of shoplifting on 12 occasions can be justified by proof that he has been convicted eleven times.

---

[1] Defamation Act 1961, s.22.

But any statement which alters the character of the main allegation or adds to its gravity must be proved to be true or the defence will fail.

Justification is a powerful and far-ranging defence, especially in countries like Ireland or England which have only a very undeveloped law of privacy. This makes it possible to publish stories about the intimate and family lives of well-known people with impunity, so long as they are true.

The principal difficulty with the defence of justification is not a legal one at all. The burden of proof of the truth of a story is on the person who published it. This means, in practice that a journalist must ask himself or herself not whether they believe the story to be true but whether they can prove that it is true on the balance of probabilities.

The process of legal proof may be quite different to the process whereby the journalist researches the story in the first place. In particular, where a story arises from information from a third party, the journalist must consider his informant's means of knowledge. Can the informant himself prove the truth of what he says? Is he willing to do so? If the information, as often happens, is known to the informant only at second-hand, who are the persons who can prove it by direct evidence, and are they willing to testify?

These questions are of particular relevance in commercial and gossip-column-type stories. In these cases in particular, informants are often, for their own reasons, extremely anxious that a particular story damaging to someone else should be published. But the story maybe false or incapable of proof. The informant may be malicious or unwilling to be seen to assist the media.

A further specific difficulty is posed by leaks from official sources. Again, such persons maybe anxious for reasons of their own to have a story published but absolutely unwilling to support it afterwards. In many such cases, the official source should not have been speaking to the press in the first place, under the rules of their occupation.

In circumstances such as these a prudent journalist will simply regard the informant as alerting him to the story and will then make his own inquiries to see if the facts can be established in an admissible way. Surprisingly often, no attempt is made to do this because the journalist puts too high a premium on early publication. If there is an action, the media is in a position of trying to research the story after the event, which is usually much more difficult.

There will be circumstances in which a journalist will recognise that a story is quite unprovable but still wish to publish. He may think that the story is undoubtedly true and the injured party will not sue. This is a calculated risk which cannot usually be recommended.

Another technique sometimes employed in these circumstances is to put the story to the person who is the subject of it and publish it in the form of reporting that person's denial. In these circumstances it is hoped that any action by the injured party can be defended on the basis of *consent* (see below). A well-informed or well-advised person will rarely make any comment in answer to an unattributed allegation of this kind and a reaction of "no comment" will not, of course, justify the publication of the allegation about which that person has declined to comment.

A decision to plead justification is a serious one because if it is unsuccessfully pleaded it will almost certainly increase the damages and costs and may assist the plaintiff in seeking aggravated or punitive damages.

On the other hand, once justification is pleaded it puts the truth of the matters alleged in the forefront of the issues to be tried and entitles the defendant to discovery against the plaintiff in relation to that issue. Discovery is dealt with in more detail elsewhere but for present purposes it means that the defendant is entitled to seek from the plaintiff a list of all documents in his possession or power which bears on the issue of truth and, subject to any claim of privilege, is later entitled to demand their production.

Discovery is of course a powerful weapon in seeking to establish the truth of a particular story. Sometimes one finds that justification is pleaded on comparatively slight grounds because the media defendant hopes that he will get the material he needs to prove the truth of the story by this means. But this hope is frequently disappointed. Particularly if the allegation relates to personal conduct, it is quite unlikely that there will be documentary proof. Discovery is of most use in commercial cases which, of their very nature, tend to generate documents.

When a media defendant pleads justification, the plaintiff becomes entitled to full and detailed "particulars" of the plea. The case of *Cooney v. Browne*[2] established that the plaintiff is entitled to be told

---

[2] [1985] I.R. 185, 190

(a) which part of the story will be alleged to be fact, as opposed to comment and (b) each and every fact which the defendant proposes to prove to establish the plea of justification. The plaintiff is not entitled to be told the evidence whereby these facts will be proved.

The effect of this decision is that before the pleadings close, and therefore before the defendant can usually get discovery, he must pin his colours firmly to the mast by stating that he will prove justification and the facts which he intends to prove in order to do so.

Criticisms of Justification: The present law of justification has been opened to criticism from both a plaintiff's and a defendant's point of view. The plaintiff may think that it is unfair that the defence can be used to justify the publication of intimate personal, sexual or family matters even though the evidence may have been obtained very intrusively. Media defendants may consider that it is unfair that the onus of proof rests on them and that a politician or other prominent figure can simply remain dumb and decline to comment on allegations that they believe to be true. It is however difficult to see how the onus of proof could fairly be changed because of the inherent difficulties for a plaintiff in "proving" a negative proposition.

Fair Comment

This is perhaps the most far-reaching defence of all. It is the means whereby the law vindicates the constitutional rights of citizens "to express freely their convictions and opinions" in relation to matters of public interest. Unfortunately, it is an area of the law which presents many conceptual difficulties and an understanding of it is not helped by the difficult nature of some of the terminology involved.

The general principle is this. There is a right to publish a sincere, comment made without malice, on a matter of public interest, so long as it is grounded on facts which are substantially true and which are stated or at least indicated in the publication complained of. Each element of this definition needs explanation.

Comment: This defence applies to comment, as opposed to statements of fact. A comment is a statement of opinion on facts. To avail of this defence, the statement must be such as an ordinary reasonable person would recognise as a comment, as opposed to a statement of fact. Thus, in a sense, the law gives legal expression to the old journalistic adage that "comment is free but facts are sacred".

Quite frequently, it may be difficult to distinguish between fact and comment. However it is important to do so because the scope for defending a comment is much greater than that available in defending the publication of defamatory fact, which must be shown to be true. If there is ambiguity as to whether a particular publication is a comment or a statement of fact, it is likely to be regarded as fact because, in the words of a leading case, "comment in order to be justifiable is fair comment must appear as comment and must not be so mixed up with the facts that the reader cannot distinguish between what is report and what is comment".[3]

Sometimes indeed, the same form of words maybe either fact or comment depending on its context. If a writer says that "the minister is taking bribes and is therefore unfit to hold office", the first statement is clearly one of fact and the second is a comment based on it. But if he merely says "the minister is unfit to hold office" without making it clear what facts this is based on, the statement can only be regarded as a statement of fact which must be justified.

Equally, what appears to be a statement of fact may be capable of defence as a comment if it is accompanied by other facts and is a deduction or conclusion come to by the writer from those other facts.

Whether any particular statement is a fact or a comment is a matter for the jury in a High Court action.

"Fair": The use of the word "fair" is hallowed by tradition but it is gravely misleading. In order to avail of the defence, it is not necessary that a writer's comment should be fair in the ordinary sense of balanced, moderate, or dispassionate. It is only necessary that it represent his honest opinion and that it is made without malice. If these conditions are met, then the comment is fair in law even though it is wrong-headed and prejudiced: the defendant has only to show that the comment is one which might be made by an honest person "however prejudiced he may be, however exaggerated or obstinate his views".[4] In the language of one of the leading cases

---

[3] *Hunt v. Star* [1908] 2 K.B. 319.
[4] *Merivale v. Carson* [1887] 20 Q.B.D. 275, freequently affirmed and adopted.

"the basis of our public life is that the enthusiast, or the crank, may say what he honestly thinks just as much as the reasonable man or woman who sits on the jury".[5]

The foregoing quotations exemplify just how broad this defence is. So far from requiring fairness in the ordinary sense, it is positively designed to accommodate the expression of extreme, foolish or prejudiced views as well as those of a more moderate kind.

An important qualification to the breadth of the defence is that the views must actually be those sincerely held by the person who expressed them. This does not usually give rise to comment where the view is the journalist's own. However, if a media defendant has repeated the comment of some other person, its defence is only as good as it would be if the action were against the original speaker. Thus, if a newspaper decides to report a strongly-worded comment by a politician, it will usually be necessary in the event of an action to be able to call the politician to give evidence of the comment representing his actual opinion. Such a witness might, of course, be subject to damaging cross examination.

Exception: Where the effect of a comment is to allege a corrupt or dishonourable motive, a defendant must go further than showing that view opinion was honestly held. He must show that it was an opinion or influence which might reasonably be held based on the facts stated or indicated. The effect of this exception is to place comments of this kind in a position midway between justification and the usual case of fair comment. If corrupt or dishonourable motives are imputed the defendant must be able to demonstrate that this is a reasonable conclusion from the facts. He need not go so far as to show that it is the only reasonable conclusion. This position is law was recently reaffirmed in the High Court in the case of *Foley v. Independent Newspapers (Ireland) Ltd.*[6]

"Grounded in fact": The comment must have a basis in fact, and this basis must be stated or indicated in the article. This is the principle limitation on the defence. As one authority puts it:

"In order to give room for the plea of fair comment the facts must be truly stated. If the facts upon which the comment

---

[5] *Silkin v. Beaverbrook Newspapers* [1958] 1 W.L.R. 743.
[6] [1994] 2 I.L.R.M. 61.

porports to be made do not exist, the foundation of the plea fails. If the defendant misstates the facts and then proceeds to comment on them he destroys the possibility of the comment being fair."

It is important to note that the omission of a relevant fact may amount to misstatement.

It is not necessary that the facts be such as prove the comment to be true, or as leave no other conclusion open. It is sufficient if they are *capable* of supporting the comment made, even though not every person who knew the facts would come to the same conclusion. Actually, the rationale of the defence of fair comment, and in particular of the requirement of the facts must be stated or indicated, is that the reader has the opportunity of judging for himself whether or not the facts support the comment.

The requirements for the facts to be truly stated or indicated in the article is the weak point of this defence from a media defendant's point of view. Time and time again a publication which might be defensible fails to meet the requirement of this defence because the facts have not been properly researched.

The phrase "stated or indicated" is also of importance. In some case the facts will be fully stated and this full statement will be immediately followed by the comment. More common, perhaps, is the situation where the facts are briefly referred to or summarised. In some instances, where the facts are thought to be very well-known, there maybe only a brief reference to them. For example, a journalist might write that "the evidence at the beef tribunal shows" that a particular person had behaved badly. This, in fact, is a form of shorthand designed to call to mind facts which, the writer hopes, are sufficiently well known to the general public as to make it unnecessary to state them fully. In such a case it would be for the jury in a High Court action to find whether the facts are stated with sufficient particularity.

Exception: There is a most important exception to the rule in that the comment must be based on facts truly stated or indicated. This is where the comment is made on facts stated in privileged circumstances, *e.g.* a Dáil report or a court judgment. In commenting on such a thing, the media is entitled to assume that what is stated is true and will have a defence of fair comment if the comment would be fair assuming the facts stated under privilege were true.

This is a most important exception because there is, of course, no control over what a deputy or senator may say in the Oireachtas, or over what a witness may say in court. Comment can be made on such a statement on the assumption that it is true. The statement must however be fairly and accurately reported and must be attributed to the person who made it.

The Scope of Fair Comment: The defence of fair comment has a very broad application, as broad indeed as the scope of "public interest". It is however of particular utility in certain instances. Comment on public affairs, on legal affairs, and on literary or artistic works offered to the public are prominent amongst them. It is an interesting observation that a media defendant will often lose a case because it has stated something as a fact, whereas a statement to much the same effect couched as a comment would be perfectly defensible. For example, where an opinion is attributed to an unnamed source it may be actionable and the newspaper maybe defenceless because it is not able to call, or name, the person who made it. The same comment presented as the writers or newspapers own might be covered by this defence.

On a Matter of Public Interest: The defence of fair comment is restricted to matters of public interest and has no application outside that sphere. It is important to bear this limitation in mind. For example, if a person publishes a book or produces a play, he is therefore entering the public domain of comment or criticism. But the comment or criticism is protected only if it relates to the act of public interest: an attack on the authors private character will not normally be defensible under the guise of criticism. The scope of public interest is broad indeed.

Matters of public interest: The following things have been expressly held to be matters of public interest:

(a) political and governmental matters;

(b) ecclesiastical matters;

(c) the administration of justice;

(d) the management of publicly funded or supported companies, bodies or institutions;

(e) artistic works offered to the public such as books, paintings, films and musical performances;

(f) newspapers and media productions publicly disseminated;

(g) local government matters;

(h) public enquiries;

(i) the public conduct of a person who holds public office, or a candidate.

This list is not, and cannot be, complete because anything which may fairly be said to invite comment and anything which is brought before the public by the person who later becomes the plaintiff may be commented upon. The scope of "matters of public interest" is extremely wide and expanding.

However, the mere fact that a person has invited public attention in some way, *e.g.* by standing for election or publishing a book does not mean that he is open to every kind of criticism. It is not open to a writer under the guise, *e.g.* of a book review to attack the private character of the author or to libel him in some way which is only tenuously connected to the work in respect of which he is invited public attention.

Without Malice: Malice is a topic of great importance in the law of defamation. Its relevance here is that proven malice will deprive a defendant of the defence of fair comment. The onus of proof of malice is on the plaintiff who alleges it.

Malice in the context of fair comment, arises when the defendant uses the right which he has to make a comment on the matter of public interest, not for the purpose of bona fide comment but for some indirect or wrongful motive. Usually, this motive will be a desire to injure the plaintiff.

If the other elements of a defence of fair comment are shown to exist, a plaintiff is taking on a heavy burden in alleging malice. The mere fact that the comment is made in extremely strong language is not in itself evidence of malice, nor is the fact that the defendant was clearly wrong in what he said. This is because the defence protects people who are unreasonable, hasty, credulous or even irrational, as well as the reasonable commentator. The real test for malice is whether the defendant actually believed the comment he made. If he did not do so, this fact will be conclusive evidence of express malice.

Since a media defendant will rarely agree that the comment did not represent his or its actual opinion, the question of malice is usually a question of *inference* from what was written. The more irrational it seems, and the smaller its basis in fact, the higher the risk that a judge or jury will conclude that it was not actually believed.

It should be noted that if the comment is sincerely believed, the mere fact that the defendant knew it would injure the plaintiff and may have wished to injure him, will not destroy the defence.

If a media defendant has a track record of attacks on the plaintiff or persons associated with him, malice may be easier to show. This might be found, for example, if the newspaper in question had previously libelled the plaintiff or published a series of scathing attacks on him.

Another significant factor is the nature of the media publication. An article which is clearly serious and well researched is at much less risk of being found to be malicious than a heavily satirical piece in a magazine known for gratuitous character assassination. In general, a media defendant will be on serious risk of being found malicious only in most unusual circumstances.

It follows from the broad scope of the defence that malice will not be proved merely from the fact that the journalist was careless in his research so that he failed to discover matters which proper research would have brought to light. There is a question of degree involved here: if the failure to research is so extreme that it strikes a judge or jury as wilful, malice may be inferred.

Privilege

Privilege is a recognition by the law that there are circumstances in which a person should be allowed to communicate material even though it later transpires to be false. Occasions of privilege are occasions where the law recognises that the public or social interest in freedom of speech takes precedence over an individual's right to have his or her reputation protected. Privilege may be absolute or qualified. In the case of absolute privilege, applying for example to a deputy in the Dáil, the person protected by that may say absolutely anything he likes and still be absolutely protected: neither falsity nor malice nor carelessness deprives him of the protection. In the case of qualified privilege, as the term suggests, the privilege is qualified in the sense that certain conditions apply to it.

Absolute Privilege

Absolute privilege is based in the Constitution or statute law. It applies to:

(a) the President in the discharge of the powers and functions of her office;

(b) members of either house of the Oireachtas speaking in the House;

(c) all official reports of the Oireachtas or of either House thereof; utterances made in the House "wherever published";

(d) publications of the Oireachtas;

(e) fair and accurate reports in a newspaper or broadcast of legal proceedings in Ireland or Northern Ireland.

It is important to note the exact parameters of these occasions. A statement in the Dáil is privileged and any report of it remains privileged wherever published. But if a person aggrieved calls on the deputy in question to "repeat those words outside" so that he can sue for them, and the deputy obliges, the privilege is lost. Equally, the court reporting privilege is confined to newspapers and broadcasts published "contemporaneously with such proceedings" and therefore does not apply to books or quarterly magazines for example. Similarly, the position of witnesses before certain committees of the Houses of the Oireachtas is probably not within the constitutional privileges of the Oireachtas; certainly it has not been the practice of chairpersons of certain committees to warn witnesses that what they say may not be privileged whereas what the Oireachtas members of the committee say is certainly privileged.

In these circumstances it is important to bear in mind that a publication outside the limit of absolute privilege may nonetheless attract qualified privilege, as outlined below. This is because, long before the arrival of absolute privilege by virtue of the constitutional or statutory provisions, the conduct of the State's political or judicial business, and reports of it, were privileged at common law.

Qualified Privilege

Qualified privilege is defence of very broad scope but its application to media libels is a limited one. The reason for this lies in the nature of the defence itself. But the occasions where qualified privilege does apply to the media are important ones and, in addition, there are specific statutory occasions of qualified privilege created specifically for the benefit of the media.

Nature of Qualified Privilege: The law recognises that there are some circumstances in which a person is entitled to say what he thinks even though it is defamatory and turns out to be untrue or at least unprovable. It defines these circumstances by reference to a concept of *duties*: the speaker must have a duty or interest in saying what he does and the person or body to whom he addresses himself must have a reciprocal duty or interest to hear it.

The nature of these duties and interests are not narrowly defined or limited. They may be legal, social or moral duties and may arise in very disparate circumstances. Thus, for example, a person is entitled to tell the gardaí about a suspicion that another person has committed a crime even though the other person transpires to be completely innocent. A parent is entitled to warn a child about one of his companions. A banker or an employer is entitled to give their actual opinions when asked for a reference even though that opinion may be mistaken.

Limited Scope

It will be seen that the foregoing examples all relate to private communications. I am entitled to tell the gardaí about my suspicions of a particular person but I am not entitled to publish them in the newspapers. The parent can tell his or her child of his reservations about a particular companion but cannot broadcast it to the world at large. This is because the person to whom it is addressed must have a duty or and interest in receiving it which is special to himself. If, however, an allegation is published in the newspaper it will necessarily be read by a large number of people who have no special duty or interest in hearing it and therefore the privilege will usually be lost.

Newspapers and Privileged Communications: It frequently happens that a newspaper becomes aware of a defamatory allegation made privately, whether through a leak or otherwise. Consider the example given in a previous chapter about Mr Smith the suspected heroin dealer who is a teacher. If a person has grounds to suspect him of heroin dealing, communicates this suspicion without malice to his headmaster or the school's board of management, this communication will attract qualified privilege. It will do so because the headmaster or board of management has both a duty and an interest to consider the facts of the case so as to determine whether Mr Smith should be allowed to continue teaching in their school. But if the private communication comes to the attention of a newspaper, there will be no privilege in its publication there because it will come to the attention of many thousands of people with no legal interest in the matter. If the allegation is untrue it will obviously constitute an appalling injustice to Mr Smith. It is for this reason that the defence of qualified privilege is of limited utility towards the media.

It is not possible to give a comprehensive statement of the circumstances in which qualified privilege may arise because everything depends on the detailed circumstances. Usually, they feature a person who is either acting under legal social or moral duty, seeking redress for aggrievance, or replying to an attack. In the last example especially, privilege may attach to a newspaper publication.

The person whose character is attacked is entitled to defend himself and to that end he is entitled to make *relevant* defamatory statements about the person who attacked him. If the attack is made in public, the response may also be public. Accordingly, especially where the attack was printed or broadcast in the mass media the response may be published there as well, with privilege where any relevant defamatory statements.

In an Irish case in 1938 it was stated that "where a person publishes in a public newspaper statements reflecting on the conduct or character of another, the aggrieved party is entitled to have recourse to the public press for his defence and vindication. . . ."

The privilege of the attacked person will then attach not only to him but to the newspaper or other organ which publishes his response.

There are however two significant qualifications. The first is that a public and defamatory response to an attack which was made only to a small number of people will not attract privilege. The second is that the privilege applies only to material which is a bona fide defence to an attack: it will not extend to an unconnected libel which is irrelevant to the attack which is rebutted.

Finally, there may be circumstances in which a publication in the newspaper, normally by advertisement, would be the only possible means of reaching all of the persons with whom an individual has a duty or an interest to communicate. Such cases would be very rare.

Media Qualified Privilege: Section 34 of the Defamation Act 1961, together with the second schedule to the Act, contains specific circumstances on which media reports have qualified privilege. These provisions are reproduced in the appendix. They provide two basic types of privilege:

(a) In respect of fair and accurate reports of proceedings in public or foreign legislatures, international organisations of which Ireland is a member or represented, the International Court of Justice foreign courts, extracts from public registers and the like; and

(b) privilege relating to fair and accurate reports of the findings or decision of certain types of bodies in the State or in Northern Ireland; the proceedings at public meetings lawfully held on matters of public concern; meetings of local authorities, statutory commissions and tribunals, reports or summaries of official notices for the information of the public by government, local authorities or the gardaí, or the equivalent in Northern Ireland. This privilege is however "subject to explanation and contradiction". This means that a person aggrieved has a right to require the publisher to publish a reasonable statement by way of explanation of contradiction: if he fails to do so adequately, the privilege is lost.

This privilege applies only to newspapers and broadcasts.

Consent

Consent is the last of what we have termed the positive defences. It is based on a very simple proposition which applies to all areas of the law: if the plaintiff has expressly, by implication, or by conduct consented or agreed to the publication of the words complained of there is a good defence. This is based on the legal principle expressed

in Latin as *volenti non fit injuria.* This means that the plaintiff's
consent (*volenti*) prevents the publication from constituting an actionable wrong (*injuria*) even though there may be actual damage
(*damnum*).

In a media context the defence of consent is likely to arise in
one of two ways. The plaintiff may actively consent to the publication
of his own words or someone else's. Thus, where the plaintiff gives
an on-the-record interview to a journalist in which he refers to or
answers, allegations defamatory of him he is probably consenting to
publication of the whole interview. This is because he knows he is
speaking to a journalist and must be taken to consent to the
publication. The position will be different if he declines to comment
on allegations or, of course, if he deals with them "off-the-record".

The second instance is where a person agrees in advance to the
publication of the findings of a tribunal, whatever that finding may
be. This usually occurs when a person joins an association (such as
horse racing regulatory bodies) whose rules provide that complaints
will be decided by a committee and the results will be published.

In all cases, evidence of consent must be clear and unequivocal
and the consent must be to the publication of what was actually
published, and not merely to something along the same lines.

Challenges to Repeat: It sometimes happens that the person who is
aggrieved by what someone else has said has no cause of action
because, for example, the words were spoken under absolute privilege
or he cannot prove publication to a third party. In these circumstances
he may challenge the other party to "repeat those words outside",
or "in front of witnesses". While this sort of challenge has the
appearance of consent to the repetition, it appears that, at least if
he makes it clear that he is seeking the repetition so that he can
sue, the repetition will be actionable. In those circumstances a
newspaper which carried the repetition would appear to be liable.

NEGATIVE DEFENCES

In this section we consider defences which consist of negativing one
or more of the essential elements of the plaintiffs' claim. For practical
purposes these consist of allegations:

1. that the defendant did not publish the words complained of;

2. that the words complained of do not, or have not been shown to, refer to the plaintiff;

3. the words complained of have no defamatory meaning.

Non-publication

In the case of a media libel, it is usually plain to demonstration what was published and by whom. A newspaper speaks for itself in this regard and the plaintiff can easily get a tape of a broadcast. But this fact is not conclusive of the liability of any particular defendant. As we have seen earlier, a plaintiff may bring an action against any person who participated in or brought about the publication of a libel. This will include, amongst others, the proprietor, editor, writer, printer and distributor of a written libel. It will also include a person who causes the libel to be printed, *e.g.* a person who supplied the material of the defamation to the newspaper hoping or requesting that it would be published, or a person who publishes a defamatory advertisement, or forces the publication of a defamatory apology.

In these cases, any individual defendant may be able to show that it did not publish the libel in question. For example, a journalist whose by-line appears may be able to claim that he did not publish a defamatory headline or sub-head. A person who supplied the story may be able to claim that the story printed deviated from what he gave the newspaper, although the deviation would have to be substantial to end his liability. The person sued as editor may not in fact have that position or a corporate defendant may not actually be the publisher of the newspaper: this happens in many cases where a publishing company has a number of subsidiary companies which publish individual titles.

Finally, of course, there may be the case where the libel is pleaded in the plaintiff's statement of claim simply does not correspond to what was printed or broadcast.

No Identification of the Plaintiff

It is an essential part of the plaintiff's proofs that the libel should be proved to have been published "of and concerning" him. There is frequently dispute about this issue where the article complained of does not name any particular individual. This sort of dispute arises in two main situations. The first is where it is clear that one person is referred to the problem being that that person is not named. The second is where a group of people, *e.g.* "the gardaí" is mentioned and the plaintiff claims that the circumstances are such as to lead people with special knowledge to identify him as the subject of the libel.

The "non-identification" defence has been successful as in *Gallagher and Shatter v. Independent Newspapers*[7] but experience shows that it is a dangerous defence for the media defendant. If apparently honest witnesses give evidence of having identified the plaintiff on some reasonable ground, it is difficult to shake this evidence. Moreover, if the non-identification defence is persisted in throughout the hearing, and a jury find against it, they may regard it as evidence of a pettifogging attitude on the part of the newspaper. Serious thought should be given to the employment of this defence and only in the rarest circumstances should it be relied on as the sole defence.

The significance of this defence is that the media is often inclined to try to sanitise a story which it knows to be defamatory by removing references to individuals. This may work if the story is of a general kind, for example about the practices of lawyers as a class. The more specific the story, however, the more likely it is that a reasonable reader may infer the identity of a particular person. Much depends on how much other detail there is in the story. The more detail, the more risk there is of the identity being deduced. Furthermore, if a media defendant has to go into evidence it may be difficult to maintain that the story does not relate to the plaintiff unless the defence is prepared to say to whom it does relate.

The guiding principle is that it does not matter how much the plaintiff's identity is disguised so long as it can be deduced by some section of the readers.

No defamatory meaning

Very frequently, a defendant will see nothing defamatory in what he has published whereas the plaintiff, perhaps relying on innuendos, will see a clear defamation. In these circumstances it will be for the

---

[7] *Irish Times*, May 10, 1980.

judge to say whether the words are capable of a defamatory meaning; where there is a jury it will be for the latter to say whether they are in fact defamatory.

In the recent (and still unfinished) case of *Conlon v. Times Newspapers*, the defendant published a review of the film "In the Name of the Father" in which it alleged that Gerry Conlon, one of the Guildford Four, had implicated his father in a statement to the English police thereby causing him to be imprisoned for the Guildford bombings. Mr Conlon Senior, it said, had been thrown into prison on the word of his "churlish son". It further stated that the father had never forgiven his son. The defendant sought to have the action struck out on a number of grounds. One of these was that, since the review had made it clear that Gerry Conlon's statement to the English police had been a "forced confession" no rational person could think the worse of him in respect of the admittedly untrue publication. The defendants failed however to satisfy the High Court that a reasonable jury could not find these words defamatory and the case is proceeding to trial.

In considering whether to plead no defamatory meaning, a media defendant should endeavour to be realistic. There is no point in advancing a purely academic argument if the publication is such that, on a common sense construction, a defamatory meaning will almost inevitably be found. A good example is the instance given in a previous chapter about the allegation that a man had, when much younger, received "roses from Rock Hudson". While it is perfectly possible to argue that this has no defamatory meaning on a literal construction, it is most unlikely that either a judge or a jury would adopt such a literal construction. Apart from anything else, it is difficult to see why the fact would be sufficiently interesting to merit publication years later if a literal meaning was all that was intended.

7. SPECIAL DEFENCES TO DEFAMATION

We now consider a number of special defences of different kinds. These are:

1. unintentional defamation;
2. the special defence available to distributors, sometimes known as the booksellers defence;
3. accord and satisfaction;
4. the defence not the action is statute barred by reason of not having commenced within the relevant limitation period.

Unintentional Defamation

We have already seen that whether or not there has been a defamation is a question of fact, and not of intention. Accordingly, at common law, if a writer publishes a defamation of what he thinks to be a fictitious person, he is nonetheless liable to a real person of the same name. Equally, if he publishes words which are not defamatory on their face but which turn out to be defamatory by reason of an innuendo, he is liable even though he did not know the facts giving rise to the innuendo.

To mitigate the harshness of this rule the legislature has provided a defence of "unintentional defamation" by section 21 of the Defamation Act 1961. The sort of case which this defence was intended to deal with is well illustrated by the famous case of *Hulton (E.) & Co. v. Jones.*[1] In this case, a newspaper published the Edwardian equivalent of a gossip column about the activities of English people enjoying a high time in France. It referred to a man called Artemus Jones and portrayed him enjoying himself in France with a lady who was not his wife and "must be – you know – the other thing". It expressed surprise at this because Mr Jones, it said, was a church warden.

---

[1] [1910] A.C. 20.

The newspaper claimed that "Artemus Jones" was an invented name used precisely because the writer could not conceive of anybody actually having this name. There was however a person of this name, who was a barrister and churchwarden. The case went to the House of Lords and is the leading authority for the proposition that the intention of the defendant was irrelevant once it had been established that the words did in fact refer to the plaintiff. It may be noted that the paper's protestations that it had never heard of Artemus Jones may have been difficult to believe because Mr Jones had for a period of years contributed articles to the paper under his own name.

There were a number of other cases over the years leading to the introduction of the defence of unintentional defamation first in the United Kingdom and then in Ireland. The nature of the defence is that it applies to the words "innocently published" in the sense that either:

(a) the publisher did not intend to publish them about the plaintiff and did not know of circumstances by which they might be understood to have referred to the plaintiff; or

(b) the words were not defamatory on the face of it and the publisher did not know of circumstances by virtue of which they might be understood to be defamatory of the plaintiff.

In either event, however, the publisher must also be able to show that he "exercised all reasonable care in relation to the publication".

It is this latter requirement which ensures that the defence is, in practice, little used. Consider the recent Irish example, described in a previous chapter, of Mr John Browne the builder who sued the *Irish Independent*. In this case the newspaper claimed that they intended the name to be a fictitious one, and that this should have been obvious from a statement to that effect printed at the end of a long article. They also said it should have been clear that all of the names used in the articles were those of colours – Green, White and Black.

However, as the case actually ran, the newspaper did not even attempt to rely on the defence of unintentional defamation. This may have been because the slightest attempt to research the matter, *e.g.* by looking up any specialist directory or even the Dublin telephone book would have elicited the information that there was a builder of that name in the Dublin area. Furthermore, the name actually used was "Browne", in which form the word is exclusively found as a surname.

There is no conclusive definition of what constitutes "reasonable care" in these circumstances but it is usually fairly clear whether reasonable care has been exercised in any particular case. Failure to take any steps to research the question in advance will certainly not pass the reasonable care test. After that, it is a question of degree. It is probably the case that where the defamation is of a very serious nature, as it was in the *Browne* case, a relatively high standard of research would be imposed.

Where the basic criteria of unintentional defamation have been met, the publisher must take certain steps immediately if he wishes to avail of the defence. He must offer to publish a suitable correction of the words complained of and a sufficient apology.

He must also take such steps as are reasonably practicable to notify persons to whom copies have been distributed that the words are alleged to be defamatory of the plaintiff.

If the offer to publish a suitable correction and a sufficient apology is accepted, and is actually published, the publishers liability will be at an end. If the offer is not accepted, the publisher can then rely on the making of the offer as a defence in any proceedings brought or continued by the plaintiff. The defence will not however be available if the plaintiff has suffered special damage. Furthermore, if the publisher is not also the author of the offending words he must prove that they were written by the author without malice.

Where a publisher is contemplating the use of this defence, he must act "as soon as practicable" after receiving notice of the alleged defamation. His offer must be accompanied by an affidavit specifying the facts which he relies on to show that the words were published innocently. This affidavit must be absolutely full because, if the matter proceeds to litigation, no evidence other then the evidence of facts set out in the affidavit will be admissible in evidence.

Distributors' Defence

This again is a defence introduced to mitigate the harshness of the common law. At common law, any person involved in the process of publishing a libel can be sued. In practice, actions are usually brought against the company which publishes the material in question, sometimes against its editor and/or the journalists who wrote or presented the piece.

In certain circumstances, however, the plaintiff will want to sue other parties as well. This will occur in two circumstances especially. The first is where there is doubt as to the solvency of the principal publisher, or its ability to meet an award of damages. The second is where it is felt that the principal publisher is actuated by malice so that he will continue to publish regardless of what vindication the court awards the plaintiff. In these circumstances it is often thought wise to join the distributor in the expectation that a distribution company will take a more commercial attitude and will not republish material likely to be defamatory.

The nature of the distributors' defence, basically, is that it is a defence of "reasonable care". It provides a full defence to a distributor who did not know, and had no means of knowing, that a particular publication contained a libel, so long as his state of mind did not result from a lack of reasonable care.

Here again there is a lack of firm guidance as to what constitutes reasonable care. Much, of course, will depend on the nature of the publication. It is unlikely that a court would find an obligation on a distributor to read every one of the titles he distributes, especially if these come to a very large number. It would be ludicrous to suggest that there was an obligation on a distributor to read every page of every edition of the *Financial Times* before selling any copies.

However, the position may be quite different in the case of a paper or magazine which notoriously publishes libels, or in respect of which the distributor has been sued before.

Because of the uncertainties of the scope of the defence of reasonable care, a wise plaintiff will rarely sue the distributor in respect of a single defamatory publication. Instead, such a person or his solicitor may write to the distributor pointing out a libellous publication; recognising that the defence of reasonable care may exempt the distributor from liability in this instance; but pointing out that the distributor is now on notice of the fact that the publication contains a libel and may contain more libels in the future.

Accord and Satisfaction

This is a defence which applies to every cause of action but often arises in a somewhat special context in libel cases. The essence of the defence is that the plaintiff has agreed to give up his right to sue the defendant, or to continue with an action already commenced, for valuable consideration. The latter phrase means simply that he has received something of value in return for his agreement. In effect, the plea is one that the action has been settled.

In the case of defamation, this usually arises where the plaintiff (or, less commonly, his solicitor) has contacted the media organ which has published the alleged defamation and has negotiated the publication of an apology or clarification. The newspaper may regard this as a full settlement of the action, while the plaintiff may regard it as merely a mitigation (see below) which leaves him fully entitled to go on with the case.

This situation is most likely to arise where a plaintiff deals directly with the editor or a journalist, neither side using solicitors. Where solicitors are involved, any settlement is likely to be agreed in detail and reduced to writing.

As in all areas of the law, an agreement to settle an action must be a fair one: a settlement induced by misrepresentation of the facts by either party will not bind the other. This is particularly relevant in defamation cases where the plaintiff considers that the agreement has been for the publication of an apology and an agreement not to repeat the libel in question. If the defendant, through inadvertence or otherwise, repeats it subsequently the plaintiff may consider the settlement at an end.

It is of course tempting for a media defendant to deal with the plaintiff who contacts it personally in an informal and direct manner. Yet these are precisely the circumstances in which a later dispute about the terms of the settlement are most likely to arise. If at all possible a media defendant should take legal advice on the negotiations and how to formalise them, even if it is not thought appropriate to involve a lawyer directly in the negotiations.

Limitations

The Statute of Limitations 1957 provides that any action must be brought within a specified time. The precise period of time varies from one cause of action to another. In defamation the limitation period for libel is six years. In the case of an infant plaintiff, *i.e.* a person who was under the age of 18 when the libel was published, the period does not begin to run until he or she has attained the age of 18.

The limitation period will not usually be a major feature of a media libel because publication, being a public act, will usually come to the attention of the potential plaintiff quite rapidly. Different considerations may apply in the case of book or pamphlet publications, or learned journals where considerable time may elapse before the libel comes to the attention of the plaintiff. Moreover, in the case of books, the publication of a new edition or the sale of a copy long after publication may give rise to an action.

MITIGATION OF DAMAGES

We now turn to matters which, though they do not provide a full defence, may be used by a defendant to mitigate its liability to the plaintiff. These are:

1. plaintiff's bad reputation

2. disproof of malice

3. apology

Plaintiff's bad reputation

It is open to a defendant, whether or not it pleads justification, to reply on evidence of the plaintiff's general bad reputation, in the area of the plaintiff's character which is relevant to the libel. Thus, for example, if the libel alleges financial dishonesty, evidence of a reputation for loose sexual morals would not be relevant.

The rationale underlying the admission of evidence of bad reputation in mitigation of damages relates to the nature of the libel action itself. It is an action intended to protect the plaintiff's reputation, or "good name" to use the constitutional phrase, from unjust attack. If the fact is that the plaintiff had no character in the relevant area even prior to the publication of the libel it is "most material that a jury who have to award those damages should know, if the fact is so, that he is a man of no reputation"[2] This is because

---

[2] *Scott v. Sampson* [1882] 8 Q.B.D. 481.

"the damage . . . which he has sustained must depend almost entirely on the estimation in which he was previously held" (*Scott v. Sampson*).[3] In Ireland, the corresponding authority is *Kavanagh v. The Leader*.[4] Thus, in a later case, the plaintiff was a jockey who brought an action for libel on the basis of an allegation that he pulled a particular horse on two specified occasions. The defendant did not plead justification. At the trial however evidence was admitted of the plaintiff's general bad reputation for pulling horses.

It must be emphasised that this is dangerous country for a defendant, especially if justification is not pleaded. If an unsuccessful attempt is made to destroy the plaintiff's general reputation, the effect will usually be to increase the damages considerably, to support an allegation of malice by the plaintiff and perhaps to open the way to exemplary damages.

It should also be noted that the only evidence admissible under this heading is *"general evidence of bad character"*. It is not usually possible to prove in evidence specific acts which led to this general reputation. The reasoning behind this limitation is that, if evidence of specific acts were admissible, a libel case would be virtually unlimited in its scope as the defendant tried to allege and the plaintiff to rebut, innumerable specific matters. Accordingly, it is only open to a defendant to call evidence to the effect that the plaintiff has, in the relevant area a poor reputation. An exception to this is criminal convictions which may always be proved. In this connection it is important to note that Ireland has no provision similar to the English Rehabilitation of Offenders Act, whereby after certain periods of time convictions become "spent": in Ireland once a person has been convicted, mere lapse of time does not prevent a defendant from relying on such conviction.

A further rationale of the rule about general bad reputation only, is that what is admissible is evidence of the plaintiff's reputation in fact, not of the reputation the plaintiff deserves. One of the leading texts says that this distinction reflects the distinction between reputation and character.[5]

It should also be noted that, by reason of Order 36, rule 35 of the Rules of the Superior Courts, where justification is not pleaded,

---

[3] *Ibid.*
[4] Unreported, Supreme Court, March 4, 1955.
[5] *Gately on Libel and Slander* (8th ed., 1981), para. 1423.

a defendant who wants to rely on the plaintiff's character, or on the circumstances of which the libel was published, in mitigation of damages, must give at least seven days notice in writing to the plaintiff of the matters which he intends to give in evidence. This requirement may be waived by the trial judge.

The Disproof of Malice

Where a defamatory statement is admittedly false, or found to have been false, the question of damages will be the only one for the court or jury. Absence of express malice on the part of the defendant is not a defence, but evidence negativing express malice may reduce damages.

It should be noted that, in practice, it is almost impossible to run mitigation along these lines coupled with a plea of justification. In practice it is necessary for a defendant to choose one line or the other.

The sort of evidence which is admissible to disprove malice includes the following: evidence that the defendant honestly believed what he published; that he had reasonable grounds for such belief; that the plaintiff in some way contributed to his belief; or that the defendant was under some disability at the time of publication such as drunkenness or insanity. This latter form of mitigation is of course in practice applicable only to individuals.

From the list above it will be seen that there is a thin line between, *e.g.* claiming that there were reasonable grounds for the defendant's belief and justification.

It may also be proved in mitigation that the defendant was not the originator of the words complained of, but merely repeated them. This is on the basis that it is thought to be less malicious to repeat something than to originate it. However, the scope for this particular form of mitigation is limited by the fact that it is confined to evidence that the defendant was repeating what he had heard from a *named* person. If he is unwilling to name his source the statement will be treated as though the defendant had himself or itself originated it.

It may also be a mitigation that the defendant was in some way provoked by the words or the conduct of the plaintiff: again this is usually more appropriate to an individual than a corporate defendant.

Apology

The plea that an apology was made or offered is in practice the single most significant form of mitigation available to a media defendant. The pleading of an apology in mitigation has been subject over the years to various statutory provisions, and now to section 17 of the Defamation Act 1961. The apology must be made or offered to the plaintiff either before the commencement of proceedings or as soon after it as the defendant has an opportunity of doing so.

There is no doubt that a satisfactory apology promptly published or offered is the best possible mitigation in the case of an admitted libel. The question of whether an apology has been offered sufficiently promptly is, it seems, a matter of law for a judge but the general adequacy of the apology will be a matter for the jury.

Experience has shown a number of features which are of great importance in deciding the effect of an apology. Chief amongst these is the wording of the publication itself. A newspaper may prefer the word "clarification" or "statement" for various reasons. In an action some years ago a representative of an English tabloid newspaper said, in relation to the term "apology", "We do not use that word". This is an extremely short sighted point of view.

Some apologies are so ritualistically worded as to be of little use. A statement that "it has been pointed out to us by solicitors for Mr Bloggs that . . ." is virtually useless and indeed is not an apology at all because it simply states what the plaintiff or his solicitors say. An apology, to have any real chance of being accepted as serious mitigation, must be a statement by the journalist or the media organ in which it acknowledges that a defamation is false and apologises for it. Hypothetical forms of apology (". . . regret if any such imputation was taken . . .") are also generally unsatisfactory.

A well-advised plaintiff will usually require a strongly worded retraction of a falsehood and may also require some indication of how the falsehood came to be published. This is because experience shows that many readers regard a formally worded apology as simply a legal ploy. False statements are, in fact, usually published due to a failure to check or due to misinformation supplied to the media.

Position of Apology

The other major feature of an apology is the prominence in which it is published or offered to be published. A libel in the main front page headline will not be seriously mitigated by an apology consisting of a few lines at the bottom of an inside page. A well advised plaintiff will usually require firm agreement as to where the apology is to be published, the typeface of the text and headline, whether or not it is to be boxed and even about the nature of the surrounding material, *e.g.* not beside a cartoon or in the middle of reports of criminal cases.

In practice, a delay of weeks or even months will not usually exclude an apology from being considered as mitigation, especially if the delay can be explained in some way. It is difficult for a newspaper, however, to explain delay by saying that it has to investigate the facts; a court may take the view that the investigation should have taken place before publication and not after it. In a case in 1980, the judge refused to allow a jury to consider as mitigation an apology published more than two years after the libel and in the immediate run up to the hearing of the action. However a reasonable delay, *e.g.* to contact the writer and to take legal advice will be allowed.[6]

Risks of Apologies

There are a number or risks attached to the publication of an apology. The first is that an apology, depending on its precise terms, may limit a media defendant's future freedom of action. Here, a firm distinction must be made between an apology which is published as part of a settlement of the entire proceedings and an apology which is published without such a settlement, and intended to be relied on in mitigation of damages.

If an apology is published as part of a negotiated settlement then the entire action is at an end and (unless there are other actions arising from the same publication) a defendant need not consider the effect of the apology on the action. In such cases the only limitation on the wording of an apology is one imposed by the defendant itself, *viz.* just how far is it prepared to go to meet the plaintiffs demands. Experience shows that media defendants generally will not publish an apology which suggests negligence on its own part or on the part of its staff even where this is the actual reason

---

[6] *Egan v. Hibernia, Irish Times,* August 17, 1980.

for the publication of the libel. Again, the plaintiff's demands as to the positioning of the apology may prove too much for the media defendant. Experience shows that, usually, newspapers are extremely reluctant to publish an apology on the front page, even where the defamation has been printed there.

If the defendant is willing to apologise in principle, but unwilling to meet the plaintiff's specific demands so that there is no settlement, the second apology situation arises. This is the case of an apology printed without agreement in the hope of mitigating damages. Here, the media defendant has to tread a thin line. If the apology printed or offered acknowledges the falsity of the original publication or some part of it, it may be impossible to plead justification, even if evidence of justification later comes to light. On the other hand, if the apology does not acknowledge the falsity of the original publication in whole or in part, and this is later established in court, the failure to acknowledge falsity may prevent it being regarded as a significant mitigation.

All these matters emphasise the necessity, which is explored in detail elsewhere, for a media defendant, at the earliest possible stage, to ask the questions "Is it true?" and "can we prove it?".

A further risk involved in the publication of an apology is that the apology itself may contain a defamation. Here, the most likely person to be defamed is the journalist who wrote the article. Other people may also take the exception, for example, where the withdrawal of an allegation against one person may suggest that another person must have done what was originally alleged against the first.

As referred to above the well known writer Honor Tracy successfully sued the *Daily Telegraph* in the 1950s over an apology it had published in respect of an article written by her (*Tracy v. Kennsly Newspapers Ltd*).[7]

However, qualified privilege comes into play here since a newspaper which has published a statement which it acknowledges to be false and defamatory is regarded as being under a moral duty to correct it. It follows from this that the publication of the apology is an occasion of qualified privilege. Accordingly a defamatory implication in an apology which is reasonably necessary for the correction, in a convincing manner, of the libellous statement will be privileged.

---

[7] *The Times*, April 9, 1954.

In recent times it has become increasingly common for a newspaper to offer an aggrieved person a "right of reply". A television broadcaster may in certain circumstances be compelled to offer a right of reply.

A right of reply will often be offered where the media organ involved considers that the article complained of is wholly or largely comment. Out of fairness to the complainant, or for other reasons, it may offer the person who complains a right or an opportunity to put his side of the case.

The acceptance of a right of reply does not of itself extinguish the complainant's right to bring an action for libel: this would have to be expressly agreed. Moreover, a right of reply does not operate as an apology, since it is merely an opportunity to put the other side. The essence of an apology is that it withdraws or disclaims the libel, and expresses regret on the part of the publishers.

8. CONTEMPT OF COURT

Contempt of court is dreaded by many journalists, but it is only vaguely understood. There is good reason for this. Contempt may be committed in a number of different ways, some quite unrelated to the others. No sooner does a lay person think he is beginning to understand one aspect of contempt of court, than he reads about another and completely unrelated one. Naturally this gives rise to confusion.

The Scope of Contempt

All of the laws and rules which constitute the law of contempt exist to protect the administration of justice and to frustrate those who obstruct it or interfere with it. The mischiefs that the law is concerned to prevent are very various, and some are of more interest to journalists than others. The subjects of the law of contempt vary from physical interference with court hearings themselves to prejudicing proceedings by publicity, "scandalising" the courts, interfering with or pressurising litigants, judges or jurors, to interfering with persons under the protection of the courts. These things, broadly speaking, constitute criminal contempt and expose those who commit them (called a contemnor) to criminal penalties. The law of contempt also has a civil aspect which usually arises where there is disobedience to an order of the court by a party to proceedings.

Legal status of contempt

Criminal contempt is a common law misdemeanour punishable by fine and imprisonment at the discretion of the court. The object of this branch of the law of contempt, like the criminal law in general, is punitive and deterrent. In civil contempt on the other hand the purpose of the law is not punitive but "coercive": its object is to compel the party to comply with the order of the court.[1]

---

[1] See *Keegan v. de Burca* [1973] I.R. 223.

CRIMINAL CONTEMPTS

The recognised forms of criminal contempt are:

(a) Contempt in the face of the court.

(b) Scandalising the courts.

(c) Pre-judging the proceedings (breaching of the *sub judice* rule).

Contempt in the face of the Court

This aspect of contempt relates to unlawful acts committed physically in a court-room, in its immediate vicinity, or in a way which is so immediately and intimately connected with a court hearing that the court will take personal knowledge of it. The eminent English judge, Lord Denning, expressed the significance of this kind of contempt in the following words:

> ". . . The phrase contempt in the face of the courts has a quaint old-fashioned ring about it; but the importance of it is this: of all the places where law and order must be maintained it is here in these courts. The course of justice must not be deflected or interfered with. Those who strike at it strike at the very foundations of our society. To maintain law and order the judges have, and must have, power at once to deal with those who offend against it. It is a great power – a power instantly to imprison a person without trial – but it is a necessary power".

The most obvious form of contempt in the face of the court is an assault on a judge sitting as such in court. A juror is equally protected.

Assaults, threats or intimidation of other people connected with the proceedings in court or going to and from court is similarly a contempt in the face of the court. Thus, threats to parties, witnesses barristers or solicitors in court or going to or from it, have been held to be contempts. Typical of this sort of thing is an Australian case where one party said to another in an elevator in a court building: ". . . You know what's going to happen to you, you bastard".

Similarly, disorderly behaviour in court, whether by way of making some form of protest or of insulting those concerned in the case is a contempt in the face of the court.

Examples of this are very various and include stripping in court, lighting a cigarette there, shouting slogans, singing songs and all forms of disorderly behaviour.

Recording of court proceedings, whether by tape, photography or video recording is a matter within the discretion of the court. In Ireland, the general tendency has been not to permit such things. There have been exceptions: the Supreme Court allowed itself to be filmed for a few moments at the sitting of the court before the hearing of a very important constitutional case and, where the parties can afford it, proceedings have been allowed to be contemporaneously recorded by a computer-linked apparatus which, seconds later, produced a transcript on screens used by the lawyers. There is no statutory law in this area and it is entirely a matter for the discretion of the individual judge or judges. Although there has been discussion about the idea of televising court proceedings there is no move imminent on the matter. It is widely believed that the experience of the O.J. Simpson criminal trial has lessened enthusiasm for the notion. Breach of the court's rules on this subject can constitute contempt.

Contempts by particular persons

Advocates   An advocate can commit contempt of court if he or she behaves in such a manner as to obstruct the court's proceedings or insult it gratuitously. This is a difficult area because a lawyer is often called upon to represent his client quite robustly and to complain in strong terms if necessary about an apparent injustice being done to him. In discharging this function the advocate is entitled to be forceful, to insist on his client's case being properly put and to protest against any step which prevents this occurring. But he cannot disobey a direct order of the court, or persist with an argument when directly ordered not to do so. Such things are best dealt with on appeal or by judicial review. Nor should an advocate be gratuitously insulting to the individual judge or the court system.

It is 40 years now since an advocate was committed for contempt of court (and on that occasion subsequently received an apology).

It is a contempt of court falsely to represent oneself as a barrister or solicitor for the purpose of representing a party in court.

Witnesses It is obvious that all of the types of contempt set out above may also be committed by a witness. However there are considerations peculiar to persons called as witnesses which can be of direct relevance to journalists.

In general, a witness who, without lawful excuse refuses to be sworn, disobeys an order of the court (*e.g.* for witnesses to remain outside until they give evidence) or refuses to answer a relevant question commits contempt. A witness, other than the defendant in a criminal case, has a privilege against self-incrimination. If he invokes this it is for the judge to decide whether there are, in fact, reasonable grounds for him to fear that he will become the subject of criminal charges.

The most sensitive area in relation to contempt by witnesses is that of refusing to answer proper questions. Various categories of persons have claimed a privilege to refuse to answer particular questions. Lawyers are in certain circumstances entitled to claim legal professional privilege. There is equally a restricted recognition of a sacerdotal privilege as between priest and parishioner. It is possible that a person, including a lawyer or clergyman, may be able to assert that a confidence was imparted to him for the purpose of bringing about a settlement of the proceedings. In such circumstances, it would appear to be open to claim the privilege attaching to "without prejudice" communications, though this privilege would presumably be the privilege of the litigant rather than the person confided in.

Journalists have claimed the right to refuse to reveal confidences or to disclose sources of confidential information. In *Re O'Kelly*,[2] an R.T.É. journalist was called as a prosecution witness in a trial before the Special Criminal Court. Mr Seán McStíofán was charged with membership of an unlawful organisation. The journalist gave evidence that he had had an interview with a man and had tape-recorded the interview. He identified the tape in court. He was then asked to state who was the man he interviewed but refused to answer on the grounds that to do so would be a breach of confidence "between me and a client which I feel, were I to breach that confidence, I would not only be putting my own exercise as a journalist into jeopardy, I would be making it very difficult adequately

---

[2] 108 I.L.T.R. 97.

for any journalist all over Ireland to promote the public good by fostering the free exchange of public opinion".

The journalist was sentenced to three months imprisonment for contempt of court. He was, in fact, released on bail pending appeal, and the appeal was confined to sentence only. In the event he did not have to serve the balance of the sentence.

However, the case constitutes a strong assertion by the Court of Criminal Appeal that "insofar as the administration of justice is concerned, the public has a right to every man's evidence, except for those persons protected by a constitutional or other established and recognised privilege".

The judgment does, however, recognise that:

> ". . . There may be occasions when different aspects of the public interest may require a resolution of a conflict of interests which may become involved in the disclosure or non-disclosure of evidence, but if there be such a conflict, then the sole power of resolving it resides in the courts. The judgement or the wishes of the witness shall not prevail. This is the law which governs claims for privilege made by the executive organs of the State or by their officials or servants, and journalists cannot claim any greater privilege."

It should be noted that the *O'Kelly* case was not in fact a strong one for the exercise of a claim to journalistic privilege, because there was no element of confidentiality in the giving of the original interview.

It should also be noted that the court did not find that a journalist would have to be compelled to answer any question simply because it was put. It specifically envisaged circumstances in which there might be a conflict between different aspects of the public interest which the court would have to resolve. This is, in fact, the approach which the courts take in relation to other kinds of confidential though not privileged information such as disclosures to a doctor, a psychologist or marriage counsellor. There, the tendency is not to compel such a witness to answer a question on a confidential and sensitive matter unless it is clearly required in the interests of justice that he should do so. In such circumstances the court will consider the importance of the issue at stake from the point of view both of the confidentiality of the relationship and of its significance to the proceedings. To take two extremes. If it appeared that an answer to a question as to who disclosed certain information was vital to the defence of a person accused of a criminal offence, it is difficult to imagine that an answer would not be required. On the other hand, if the purpose of the question was simply to test the credibility of the witness, which could be achieved in some other way, an answer might not be required.

In all cases, it is necessary that the relevance of a question be established before any question of contempt can arise.

There has been no case in the Superior Courts since *O'Kelly* in which the specific position of journalists has been tested. It is suggested, however, on the basis of the last cited passage from the judgment in that case, and on the basis of not dissimilar *dicta* in the jurisprudence of the European Court of Human Rights, that an approach of balancing the competing interests on a case by case basis will probably be adopted if the question again comes before the courts.

The English Contempt of Court Act 1981 provided that:

> ". . . No court may require a person to disclose, nor is any person guilty of a contempt of court for refusing to disclose, the source of information contained in a publication for which he is responsible, unless it is established to the satisfaction of the court that disclosure is necessary in the interests of justice or national security or for the prevention of disorder or crime."

While this provision does not, of course, apply in Ireland, it is not dissimilar to the approach which, it is suggested, the Irish courts might adopt.[3]

At present, refusal to answer a question is treated as a criminal contempt. As with all criminal contempts, it is punishable by imprisonment for a fixed period. This contrasts with imprisonment for civil contempt which may be indefinite since it is to last until the defendant complies with the court's order. In *Keegan v. de Burca*[4] a dissenting judgment in the Supreme Court suggested that contempt consisting of refusal to answer a question

> "is an offence which continues as long as the refusal continues and cannot adequately be measured while the offence contin-

---

3 See also the discussion of *X. v. Morgan Grampian (Publishers)* below.
4 See n.1.

ues; if dealt with by a fixed sentence, the sentence might be
oppressive on the offender whereas a sentence which ends when
the offence ceases and the contempt is purged cannot be
oppressive. It is not the declaration of refusal to answer the
question, but the refusal to comply with the requirement which
is the gist of the offence. Furthermore, in a case such as this
the purpose of the sentence is not primarily punitive but
coercive".

Although this was a dissenting judgement it appears to have a
great deal of logical force.

Parties Parties – the plaintiff or defendant in a civil case or the
defendant in a criminal case – are capable of committing any of the
forms of contempt mentioned above, and the same rules apply to
them.

There are, however, particular kinds of behaviour which, on the
basis of experience, are peculiar to the parties, notably in criminal
cases. In particular, there have been cases of constant interruption
of the proceedings so that it is impossible for them to continue. In
such instances, apart from proceedings for contempt, the court has
power to remove the offending party from a courtroom. Where this
has happened in recent times, defendants in criminal cases have
been brought to a room with an audio-link to the court so that they
can hear, but not directly participate in, the proceedings.

Outbursts by defendants quite frequently occur in criminal cases
after conviction or sentence. Although such things are capable, clearly
of constituting a contempt of court, they will usually be ignored by
the presiding judge. Apart from anything else, if a significant sentence
of imprisonment is being imposed in any event, there is little point
in adding to it the relatively short sentence which a contempt
normally attracts. Similarly, outbursts by relatives of defendants or
victims and their relations may simply be ignored when not persistent.
In this area the discretion of the court is paramount.

Jurors Jurors may also commit contempt in any of the ways
mentioned above. Proceedings against jurors from contempt are rare.
However, the Juries Act 1976 contains a provision for a variety of
summary offences which can be committed in connection with jury
service.

Scandalising the Court

The risk of contempt by scandalising the court is one to which journalists and publishers are particularly, but not uniquely, liable.

The offence of contempt of court by scandalising the court is committed by publishing material calculated to bring a court or a judge of a court into contempt, or to lower his authority, thereby endangering public confidence in the court and thus obstructing and interfering with the administration of justice.

However, the offence is emphatically not committed by mere criticism or disagreement, however emphatic, with what has been decided by a court.

In practice, the Irish cases show that the offence will not be committed unless there is an attribution to the court of corrupt, dishonest or unlawful behaviour or total and unreasoned arbitrariness.

Furthermore, the attack must be on a judge in his official capacity because:

> ". . . In his personal character a judge receives no more protection from the law than any other member of the community at large. . . ." (*R. v. McHugh*).[5]

It is obvious from the foregoing brief summary that lying between contempt and legitimate criticism may be difficult to decide in borderline cases. to decide in borderline cases. The reported judgments provide some guidance as to what the courts have regarded as contempt.

In *Attorney General v. O'Ryan and Boyd*[6] a letter was published in a newspaper attacking a judge who had jailed rioters despite a plea for leniency by a local priest. The judge was a protestant and the letter suggested, amongst other things, that the result would have been different if the plea for leniency had "come from the local lodge of the Grand Orient and embossed with a square and compass". The High Court held that ". . . It is unnecessary . . . to point out how offensive such a statement was and how the suggestion, that the judge could be so swayed, was calculated to injure him and his court in the eyes of the public."

---

[5] [1902] 2 I.R. 82.
[6] [1946] I.R. 70.

In *Re Kennedy and McCann*[7], a tabloid newspaper published a "biased and inaccurate" account of custody of children proceedings in the High Court which had led to custody being awarded to their father. This, in any event, was a contempt of court since it identified the children by name, contrary to statutory provisions providing for privacy of such proceedings. However, it also contained gross misstatements as to the reasons for the decision and concluded that ". . . It seems that money and the lifestyle it could buy was regarded by the courts was by far the most important consideration. . . ." It also suggested that justice could not be obtained in Irish courts and, accordingly, that Ireland was a "sick society".

The Supreme Court held that ". . . in this instance there has been a contempt of a serious nature. Not only was the article written in breach of an order prohibiting publication but it was a distortion of the facts and was calculated to scandalise the members of the court . . . for it imputed to them base and unworthy motives which, if substantiated, would render them unfit for their office".

It was also held that:

> ". . . the offence of contempt by scandalising the court is committed when, as here, a false publication is made which intentionally or recklessly imputes base or improper motives and conduct to a judge or judges in question. Here, the publication bears on its face, if not an intent, at least the stamp of recklessness".

In this case, the offence of contempt was admitted and apologies tendered. The court imposed substantial fines.

Similar principles were applied in two cases where the integrity of the Special Criminal Court was attacked. In *Attorney General v. Connolly*[8] comment was made in a Sinn Féin publication, about the likely outcome of the trial, for the murder of a guard, of one Henry White. The defendant was described as "fast approaching martyrdom" and it was stated that he "awaits his death, which sentence will inevitably be passed on him after his mockery of a trial before the Special Criminal Court is over".

In *Re Hibernian National Review Ltd*[9] the periodical *Hibernia*

---

[7] [1976] I.R. 382.
[8] [1947] I.R. 213
[9] [1976] I.R. 388.

published letters about the conviction of Noel and Marie Murray for the murder of a guard. In one, the word "trial" was printed in inverted commas and it was stated that ". . . they were tried without a jury and virtually without evidence. . . ." Another letter suggested that ". . . many defendants are presumed guilty until they can prove their innocence against the belief of the gardaí. In the ordinary course of events this mixture of special justice and bias towards the police is a reversal of justice. . . ." The letter also misstated the extent of the evidence against the defendants.

This case is of particular interest because the Director of Public Prosecutions' initial application for a Conditional Order of Attachment for Contempt was refused by the President of the High Court. However, the D.P.P. successfully appealed to the Supreme Court where it was held that the words meant "that the members of the Special Criminal Court conducted a travesty of a trial, that they did not give the benefit of the doubt to the accused, and that they were involved in an effort by the government and the gardaí to produce a false verdict of guilty, and that the only evidence against the accused was their own statements".

The Supreme Court, however, emphasised that criticisms of the existence of a Special Criminal Court, or of the retention at the time of a death sentence, were not in themselves a contempt of court. "These are matters which may validly be debated in public even if the comments made are expressed in strong language or are uniformed or foolish".

Some time later, the Association for Legal Justice issued a press statement commenting on the Special Criminal Court's trial and conviction in the same case. Speaking of the death sentence imposed, the Association said that it was:

> ". . . Particularly reprehensible because it was passed by the Special Criminal Court, a court composed of government appointed judges having no judicial independence which sat without a jury and which so abused the rules of evidence as to make the court akin to a sentencing tribunal. . . ."

This was held to be a contempt for similar reasons.

If, however, a publication lacks the element of attributing base, corrupt, dishonest or arbitrary motives to a judge, criticism of a judgement is entirely permissible. In *Weeland v. R.T.É.*,[10] the High

---

[10] [1987] I.R. 662.

Court considered a suggestion that R.T.É. had committed a contempt of court in a portion of a programme about certain land dealings in Cork. The relevant part of the programme dealt with the circumstances in which an action of fraud in the sale of land had been dismissed in the Circuit Court. The programme was found to have been unbalanced in its report of the Circuit Court proceedings because it made "no attempt to deal, however briefly, with the Circuit judge's analysis of the evidence, the view he took and the weight he attached to certain items of evidence in reaching his verdict".

Despite this, the programme was held not to constitute a contempt. The judge held:

> ". . . I do not see why a judgement cannot be criticised, providing it is not done in a manner calculated to bring the court or the judge into contempt. If that element is not present there is no reason why judgement should not be criticised. Nor does the criticism have to be confined to scholarly articles in legal journals. The mass media are entitled to have their say as well. The public take a great interest in court cases and it is only nature that discussion should concentrate on the result of cases. So criticism which does not subvert justice should be allowed. Even though this programme was in my opinion unbalanced in relation to the judgement on the Circuit judge, it did not pass over the boundary of acceptable limits".

Changing times

This case is not the only indication that the courts are becoming less sensitive to criticism of themselves. In *Desmond v. Glackin (No. 1)*,[11] a government minister (Mr Des O'Malley) made a comment about High Court proceedings instituted by one of those involved in a Companies Act inspectorship relating to the purchase by Telecom Éireann of premises at Ballsbridge. The proceedings had had the effect of delaying the inquiry by the inspector, who had been appointed by the Minister. Mr O'Malley, in the course of a radio interview, commented that the proceedings ". . . certainly facilitated (a particular person) in blocking the inquiry". Although it was

---

[11] [1992] I.L.R.M. 490.

suggested that this was a contempt of court the High Court found otherwise, regarding the comment as a reference to delays in the court system. This finding was despite the fact that the judge plainly did not agree with Mr O'Malley's views.

The case of *McCann v. An Taoiseach*,[12] is a most interesting one in illustrating the present attitude of the courts and the appropriate course of action for journalists who have unwittingly strayed into this form of contempt. In the course of the campaign in relation to the referendum to approve the Maastricht Treaty, the plaintiff sought a court order to prevent a broadcast by the Taoiseach. R.T.É. published a report of the case which, they subsequently admitted, was seriously inaccurate in that it attributed remarks to the judge which he had not made. Mr Justice Carney held that this constituted a serious contempt but that no action was required because (a) the error had not been intentional or malicious and (b) it had been immediately and fully repaired.

Comparing the more recent cases to the older ones, changes in attitude on the part both of the media and of the judiciary can be discerned. None of the very recent cases illustrate the kind of deliberate and strongly-worded attacks on the integrity of judges which featured quite frequently in the older cases. On the part of the judiciary, they have shown a willingness to allow a broad scope for legitimate criticism which is moderately phrased, even though the criticism may be based on inaccurate facts.

Contempt is an area uniquely for the discretion of the court and in particular it should be noted that it is open to a judge to take no action even though a contempt is clearly established. This was done on the case just quoted. It was also the course adopted by the courts in relation to the editor of the newspaper which published the letter in question of *Attorney General v. O'Ryan and Boyd*, quoted above.[13] The writer of the letter, who was a county councillor, had read the offending letter at a meeting of the county council, which had then passed a motion critical of the judge. When contempt proceedings were taken against him, the editor of the newspaper who had printed the letter by way of a report on the county council proceedings, was also accused of contempt. The editor gave evidence that he regarded the letter as wrong-headed and unfair and considered

---

[12] Unreported, High Court, June 23, 1992.
[13] See n.6.

that publishing it would indicate to a fair-minded reader that the county council's resolution had been passed in circumstances of bias and hysteria. He therefore claimed the publication was for the public benefit.

While the court was divided on the merits of this defence in the particular circumstances, all three judges agreed that no action should be taken against the editor. Mr Justice Gavan Duffy said:

> ". . . It must never be forgotten to an editor that his task in having to decide, often at short notice, whether or not to publish offensive material concerning a topic of the day, may be arduous to a high degree, and I should have much sympathy here with Mr Boyd if in the peculiar circumstances he had made an error of judgment; and I should be very slow indeed to hold that, having no personal interest in the unsavoury episode, he had by a very understandable mistake incurred the penalties of contempt of court".

Although this case is 50 years old, the approach taken to the position of the editor is consistent with the approach of the courts in more recent cases and appears to suggest that the position of a journalist who merely reports remarks, in circumstances of haste, may be more favourably regarded than that of the person who originates them.

Two other points require to be made. The Law Reform Commission in its paper on Contempt of Court has recommended that the retention of contempt by scandalising, where the alleged contempt consists of attributing corrupt conduct to a judge or court, or of publishing a false account of legal proceedings. They recommend that it should be necessary to prove intention or recklessness, and a substantial risk to the administration of justice or the judiciary being brought into serious disrepute.

Secondly, it should be noted that many remarks capable of constituting this form of contempt would also constitute a defamation of the judge or judges referred to, and such an action might be pursued regardless of whether or not contempt proceedings were taken.

Defences

Mens rea   Most serious criminal offences require the proof of mens *rea rea*, that is, a guilty mind in the sense of an intention to commit the crime in question. Curiously, it is unclear on the authorities whether this requirement applies in the case of contempt by scandalising. The better view, on the basis of *Re Kennedy and McCann*,[14] above, appears to be that intention or recklessness is required. The point is probably more of academic than practical interest because in many cases the words will be unequivocal meaning and their tendency clear, as it was in the case just cited.

Justification Again, there is little direct authority on this point, partly because in many of the cases the publications were admitted to be false by the time contempt proceedings came for hearing. However, the Supreme Court judgment in *Director of Public Prosecutions v. Walsh*,[15] included the words "baseless" in the judicial definition of the offence of contempt by scandalising and noted that it was admitted that the words complained of would amount to a criminal contempt "if untrue and baseless".

It therefore appears that truth would constitute a defence to an allegation of contempt by scandalising. There is, however, no recorded Irish case where this has been successfully pleaded.

Fair comment It follows from the definition of the offence itself that a comment which is fair, in the sense in which that term is used in the law of defamation, will not constitute a contempt of court. It is probable that the jurisprudence relating to this defence in defamation would be applied with the necessary adaptations to a defence of fair comment to contempt by scandalising.

Public benefit Although it has been suggested that maybe a separate defence to the effect that publication was for the public benefit, it is probable that this is merely an aspect which, together with other features of a particular case, might prevent a publication from being a contempt at all. In the case of *Attorney General v. O'Ryan and Boyd* above,[16] the member of the court who considered that the publication had in fact been for the public benefit gave his reasons

---

[14] See n.7.
[15] [1981] I.R. 412.
[16] See n.6.

in a form which suggests that he did not regard the publication as constituting contempt. The publication, he held, had in its context merely demonstrated the baselessness of the allegations contained in the letter which was the subject of the proceedings.

Pre-judging the proceedings of the *sub judice* rule

In all forms of proceeding, there is necessarily delay between the commission of the acts complained of, the institution of legal proceedings and the eventual verdict or judgment. Publicity during these periods can radically alter the context in which the trial takes place. For example, if the guilt or the innocence of a criminal defendant is constantly proclaimed by the media, or if selective portions of the evidence are given wide publicity, that may seriously affect the rights of the prosecution or defence, as the case may be, to a fair trial. If unrestricted comment on these matters were permitted, as it is in parts of the United States, we would also have the American phenomenon of both prosecution and defence conducting PR campaigns, leaking evidence, and generally seeking trial by media in advance of the actual hearing. Indeed, American experience has been a major factor in strengthening traditional concerns in this area.

This is possibly the most common form of contempt alleged and found against media defendants. It has been given a particular topicality by the recent upsurge in investigate reporting of criminal matters, including, notably, the publication of information alleged to come from "garda sources" but not otherwise proved.

This heading of contempt is not limited to prejudging proceedings. It may also consist of interfering with parties or witnesses by making it difficult or impossible for them to give evidence or prosecute their cases by public pressure or by disclosure of private legal information. The area also features the phenomenon of gagging writs whereby proceedings, notably for defamation, are instituted more for the purpose of stifling comment than being prosecuted to finality.

General Principle

The Constitution provides that no person shall be tried for a criminal offence except in due course of law. This involves a trial on legally admissible evidence before a jury or other tribunal which is in fact impartial and is seen to be so. Therefore, in the words of a leading English textbook:[17]

> ". . . Publications which directly or indirectly prejudge the merits of a trial and particularly those which impute the guilt or innocence of the accused are classical examples of trial by newspaper. Such publications obviously have the tendency to prejudice the fair trial of an accused, since they could clearly trade bias in the minds of those who actually have to try the case. It is therefore contempt to impute directly or indirectly the guilt or innocence of an accused before he has been tried".

It is important to note that contempt may be committed by prejudging the issues in favour of an accused in a criminal case, as well as against him. Indeed, the same publication may have both effects simultaneously on different readers. Thus, in the case of *Attorney General v. Hibernian National Review Ltd*,[18] High Court, May 16, 1972 it was held that description of a person awaiting trial as "a political prisoner", by a well-known and responsible journalist who held himself out as knowing the facts, might tend to prejudice a potential juror in favour of the accused, or against him, according to the juror's political views.

The *sub judice* rule, in the context of criminal proceedings, may be offended against in a huge variety of ways which range from the blatant to the subtle. In the 1940s, the *Daily Mirror* commenting on the arrest of a person on a charge of murder did so under the heading "The Vampire Will Suck no More". Little knowledge or sensitivity is required to discern the contempt in this. Most contempts, however, are less dramatic and have consisted of such things as asserting that an accused's alleged statement of admission had been extracted by torture; stating that a defendant in a current trial was a relation of a well-known criminal; referring to a person pejoratively in an article on organised crime published the day before the person was due to go on trial; giving details of an accused's previous convictions prior to his trial; making one-sided or inaccurate revelations of what was said to be the evidence for one side or another prior to the trial.

---

[17] *Borrie and Lowe on Contempt* at p. 100.
[18] See n.9.

Commencement of risk

A very important question for journalists is when the risk of contempt by prejudgment starts to apply. There is English and Northern Ireland authority for the proposition that it may apply when criminal proceedings are "imminent", though not actually commenced. However, this does not appear to be the law in Ireland, on the basis of *The State (DPP) v. Independent Newspapers Ltd.*[19] In that case, the defendant had reported that the gardaí were about to bring charges for sexual offences against a local authority member. Two days later such proceedings were in fact commenced. The Director of Public Prosecutions sought attachment for contempt in these circumstances but Mr Justice O'Hanlon declined to make an order. He said:

> ". . . As the courts must always have regard to the countervailing importance of preserving the freedom of the press, I do not consider that the facts disclosed in the affidavit grounding the present application or of such a character as would justify me in extending the law as to contempt of court in the manner now sought by the Director of Public Prosecutions".

However, it is clear from the report that the judge's attention was not drawn to authorities which support the proposition that the test is one of imminence, not the actual commencement of proceedings.

This is a matter which may well be litigated again, particularly in view of a spate of recent media articles plainly suggesting that a number of persons, who had not been charged with any offence at the time of writing, are in fact guilty of serious crimes.

After Trial: Appeal Pending

This situation was fully explored in the very important case of *Cullen v. Magill Publications (Holdings) Ltd.*[20] In this case Cullen had been convicted of a notorious crime. He had an appeal pending to the Court of Criminal Appeal. Before the appeal came up *Magill* magazine proposed to publish an article based on the exclusive story of the principal prosecution witness, a woman accomplice. Cullen sought

---

[19] [1995] I.L.R.M. 183.
[20] [1994] I.L.R.M. 577.

an injunction to restrain publication. He was successful in the High Court, where Mr Justice Barrington decided that there was a risk of prejudice, even though the appeal would be heard before three judges, rather than jurors. The defendants contended that this obviated the possibility of prejudice since judges were trained to exclude irrelevant material from consideration. The judge held that "In my view it is absurd to suggest that judges' minds could not be affected by prejudice".

The Supreme Court, however, found for the defendants, thereby permitting publication. The Supreme Court regarded the argument that judges might be affected in their consideration of legal arguments by publicity as "unsustainable".

This view has been trenchantly and, in the author's view, correctly criticised. The Law Reform Commission stated that "with respect this is too extreme a statement at variance with human experience". Nevertheless the case stands as strong authority for the proposition that, where a trial before a judge or judges only is anticipated, it is difficult or perhaps impossible to allege contempt in the form of prejudgment. This would exclude all civil actions, other than High Court actions for defamation, assault or false imprisonment, from the scope of this form of contempt.

Effect on a litigant or appellant

Apart from the risk that a publication prejudging the issues in proceedings may affect the tribunal trying those issues, there is also a risk that extensive publicity, particularly of the campaigning type, might have an effect by making a plaintiff, defendant or appellant feel that he had no chance of success in pursuing his case. There is no authority on this point in the reported cases.

Photographs

It is important to note that the publication of a photograph of an accused person is capable of amounting to contempt in a case where visual identification is in question. It may prejudice the accused by fostering an inaccurate identification and may also prejudice the prosecution by lessening the value of an identification witness.[21]

---

[21] See *Re McArthur* [1983] I.L.R.M. 355.

CIVIL CONTEMPT

The main difference between civil contempt proceedings and criminal contempt proceedings is that the object in civil contempt proceedings is to get a person or body to comply with a court order. From a journalist's point of view the main dangers occur where a journalist either ignores a court order, *e.g.* an injunction or reports a matter in ignorance, for example, that the material being covered has been the subject of a court order.

A person failing to obey a court order can be attached and committed. This means they can be brought before the courts and imprisoned until they purge their contempt. Because a person's liberty is at stake there are strict rules governing the procedure. These are set out in the Rules of the Superior Courts.

Generally speaking a person whose committal or attachment is being sought, will be served with a notice of motion which will contain a penal endorsement, effectively a warning that they could be sent to prison if found in contempt. Such a motion must be served on the offending person personally with a copy of the order allegedly being broken.

The court has complete discretion whether or not to order committal or attachment even in cases where the contempt is clear-cut. Generally speaking if the court is satisfied that the contempt was a genuine error on the part of a journalist an apology may suffice. This is more likely to happen where the court is happy that it would have been difficult for the journalist to know of the existence of the Order.

Protection of Journalists' Sources

The principal worry most journalists have is the extent to which they will be able to protect their sources. Journalists like to be able to assure confidential contacts that there win be no question of them revealing their source. In England the need for the protection of journalists' sources was recognised as stated above with the passing of the Contempt of Court Act 1981. Under that Act a journalist shall not be required to disclose his source unless it can be established to the satisfaction of the court that the disclosure is necessary in the interests of (a) national security, (b) justice (c) the prevention of crime or (d) the prevention of disorder. This section was tested all the way to the House of Lords, and thence to the European Court of Human Rights in *X. v. Morgan Grampian (Publishers)*.[22] In this case two associated privately owned companies prepared a business plan for the purposes of negotiating a substantial loan to raise additional working capital. A copy of the plan was stolen and a trainee journalist was contacted by a confidential source and given information about the companies including the projected loan. The trainee journalist decided to write an article on the companies and telephoned them and the bankers to check certain facts.

The companies immediately applied for an *ex parte* injunction prohibiting publication of anything contained in the draft plan. They also applied under section 10 of the Contempt of Court Act requiring the journalist to disclose the source of his information, claiming it was in the interests of justice that he do so. In finding for the companies, one of the judges stated:

> "Construing the phrase 'in the interests of Justice' in this sense immediately emphasises the importance of the balancing exercise. It will not be sufficient *per se*, for the party seeking disclosure of a source protected by s. 10 to show merely that he was unable without disclosure to exercise the legal right or avert the threatened legal wrong on which he bases his claim in order to establish the necessity of disclosure. The judge's task will always be to weigh in the scales the importance of enabling the ends of justice to be attained in the circumstances of the particular case on the one hand against the importance of protecting the source on the other hand. In this balancing exercise it is only if the judge is satisfied that disclosure in the interests of justice is of such preponderating importance as to overtake the statutory privilege against disclosure that the threshold of necessity will be reached."

The journalist lost the case but refused to identify his source or hand his notes into court and was fined £5,000. The matter went before the European Court of Human Rights who found that the English court order breached Article 10 of the European Convention of Human Rights which states:

> "(1) Everyone has the right to freedom of expression. This

---

[22] [1991] 1 A.C. 1.

right shall include freedom to hold opinions and to receive and impart information and ideas without interference by public authority and regardless of frontiers, This article shall not prevent States from requiring the licensing of broadcasting, television or cinema enterprises.

(2) The exercise of these freedoms since it carries with it duties and responsibilities, may be subject to such formalities conditions, restrictions or penalties as are prescribed by law and are necessary in a democratic society, in the interests of national security, territorial integrity or public safety, for the prevention of disorder or crime, for the protection of health or morals, for the protection of the reputation or rights of others, for preventing the disclosure of information received in confidence, or for maintaining the authority and impartiality of the judiciary."

Interestingly the court took the view that the English court order was not "necessary in a democratic society". The restriction imposed by English law was not required in any of the "interests" set out in Article 10(2). Although the decisions of the Court of Human Rights are not binding on the Member States who have signed the convention, including Ireland, its findings do, nevertheless, impact on the type of legislation a member country to the Convention might or might not enact. As Ireland does not have a Contempt of Court Act it is likely that in the event of enacting such legislation consideration would be given to the Human Rights Court's findings.

9. PLEADING AND PROCEDURE

The term pleading refers to the system of formal written documents exchanged between the parties before a case comes to court. The principal pleadings are plaintiff's summons and statement of claim, the defendant's defence and where necessary the plaintiff's reply. Either party can seek "further and better" particulars of the other's claim or defence. Allied to these is a system of discovery, notices to admit, and interrogatories which may or may not feature in any particular case.

Pleadings are, perhaps, of more importance in a libel action then in any other type of proceeding. Cases can be won or lost at the pleading stage. Proper attention to pleadings will define the issues to be tried and force a plaintiff or defendant to think out his case in a realistic way. Discovery, notices to admit facts and interrogatories, together with the power to summon witnesses, can be essential in the all important process of evidence gathering.[1]

It is therefore important for a journalist or media executive to have a sound knowledge of these matters which are too often cloaked in mystery.

Preliminary Correspondence

The great bulk of libel actions begin with a letter of complaint from a solicitor acting for an aggrieved person. This will usually demand some form of redress either in general or specific terms.

Far too often this preliminary letter elicits no reply at all. This is rarely a sound tactic: it will usually have the effect of propelling the plaintiff further towards issuing proceedings. On other occasions the preliminary letter elicits merely a civil service style holding letter, which may or may not be followed by a more substantive reply.

It is particularly undesirable to reply to an initiating letter with a statement that time is needed to investigate the complaint. Such a reply may be used at trial to suggest that the story complained of was insufficiently researched before it was published.

---

[1] See Appendix 1.

Every preliminary letter should be examined carefully and quickly along the lines indicated elsewhere in this book. If there has been a mistake or injustice, or if the letter seems to indicate a significant claim, the question of providing some redress satisfactory to the plaintiff should be considered immediately. (see Chapter 6).

If no accommodation is possible, considerable attention should be paid to correspondence. The preliminary letters and replies thereto will almost certainly be read out in court and all open correspondence should be composed with a view to that possibility. Those dealing with a complaint should have firmly in mind the distinction between open correspondence and correspondence which is "without preju-dice". This latter term refers to correspondence which is written in an attempt to settle the case and is privileged from disclosure in court, unless this privilege is waived. A letter may be "without prejudice" whether or not it is marked with these words.

All correspondence from a potential plaintiff should normally be handed to a solicitor at an early stage and its contents discussed.

Particular attention should be paid to correspondence which requires an apology, especially if the form of the proposed apology is included in the letter. It frequently happens that a media defendant is prepared to publish some form of apology or clarification, but not that required by the plaintiff. A court or jury will naturally compare and contrast the form of apology sought by the plaintiff with any apology actually published by the media defendant.

If the plaintiff demands an apology or retraction without specifying the form, consideration should be given to some form of publication acceptable to the media defendant which can, of course, be published with or without the plaintiff's consent. This may be central in mitigation of damages and may have the effect of prevailing on the plaintiff not to issue proceedings.

Plenary Summons

If the plaintiff proceeds to litigation, his first step would be the service of a plenary summons. In the United Kingdom this is referred to as a "writ" and that terminology is sometimes (incorrectly) used here. The plenary summons is purely an initiating document, and is usually very simple in form. The date of its service may be crucial because it is the date on which the statute of limitations ceases to run against the plaintiff.

The plenary summons is a formal document issued out of the Central Office of the High Court under the authority of the Chief Justice. It is titled with the name of the parties so that the defendant knows who precisely is being sued. It contains a request to the defendant to enter an "appearance" in the Central Office of the High Court within a specified number of days.

The plenary summons also contains a "general endorsement of claim". This states in very broad terms the nature of the plaintiff's claim and will often be as simple as "the plaintiff claims for damages for libel". Other claims may also be intimated such as a claim for an injunction or other causes of action such as malicious falsehood or breach of copyright. This endorsement of claim will normally be signed by the plaintiff's counsel.

Finally, the plenary summons will contain a form identifying the plaintiff and his address and the name and place of business of his solicitor.

It is of course possible for a plaintiff or a defendant to issue a plenary summons and take all the other steps in an action personally. A solicitor is, however, employed in the huge majority of cases.

Appearance

Once a plenary summons has been issued the defendant is required to enter an appearance. If this is not done the plaintiff can deliver a statement of claim and seek judgment together with an order that the damages be assessed by a judge or jury. An appearance is simply a statement that the defendant intends to defend the action and identifying the solicitor retained on his behalf.

Statement of Claim

Once the appearance is entered, the plaintiff becomes obliged to deliver a statement of claim, if he has not done so already. This is the plaintiff's principal pleading in which he sets out his case. The statement of claim is a document divided into numbered paragraphs in which the plaintiff states in detail what his case is.

It would usually commence with an identification of the plaintiff by name, address and occupation, and similar particulars in relation to the defendant. If a number of defendants are sued it will normally identify their respective roles in relation to the publication, *e.g.* proprietor, editor, writer, printer, distributor etc.

The substantial part of the statement of claim will then recite the publication complained of, identifying it by date. It must allege that the publication was "of and concerning" the plaintiff. If the plaintiff has not been named in the publication, it may give particulars of the way in which it is claimed he is to be identified as the subject of it.

The statement of claim will then allege that the words complained of are defamatory of the plaintiff. It will often do so by using a form of words such as "are grossly defamatory of the plaintiff and damaged him in his credit and reputation and exposed him to odium ridicule, contempt and distress". The statement of claim will very frequently set out the meanings which the words complained of are alleged to bear. It will often say: "said words in their ordinary and natural meaning, further or in the alternative by innuendo, meant and were understood to mean . . . ". There will then follow a list of the meanings alleged.

This aspect of the statement of claim is most important. A defendant's lawyer will look to see whether innuendo is in fact pleaded. If it is not, the plaintiff is confined to the "natural and ordinary" meaning of the words and will normally be precluded from calling evidence from witnesses who will say how they understood them. In a number of cases, the failure of the plea to innuendo has confined the plaintiff to the natural and ordinary meaning, which was then being held not to be defamatory. In the case of *Berry v. Irish Times*,[2] a failure to plead innuendo in relation to the term "felon setter" led to the plaintiffs losing the action when the courts held that the word was not defamatory in its natural and ordinary meaning.[3]

If innuendo is pleaded, it should be followed by a statement of the "facts extrinsic to the words complained of" as a result of which the innuendo arises. A statement of claim may go into detail about the loss, damage and distress allegedly suffered by the plaintiff. A statement of claim will usually allege that the words complained of were published "falsely and maliciously". This form of words may not indicate a claim of actual malice. Where actual malice is relied on details of it may be given in the statement of claim, *e.g.* that the words were published knowing them to be false or reckless as to

---

[2] [1973] I.R. 368.
3 See "Innuendo" in Chapter 4.

whether they were true or false. Other circumstances may be relied on to support the claim of actual malice.

The statement of claim may also allege that the words were published for profit, to increase the sales of the newspaper or for some other specified motive. The statement of claim will end with a claim for damages. The defendant's lawyers will be anxious to see whether the claims, in addition, aggravated or punitive damages. The statement of claim will normally be signed by the plaintiff's counsel and will be delivered by his solicitor.

Service

The plenary summons must of course be served before the defendant is properly impleaded. Most initiating letters will invite the defendant to nominate a solicitor to accept service and proceedings, and this is usually done. Thereafter, all documents can be served on the solicitors on record unless and until there is notice that their retainer has been terminated.

Service often gives rise to difficult problems for a plaintiff. In media cases, however, the identity and whereabouts of the defendant publisher and those employed by him is usually well known or easily ascertainable and problems rarely arise. Provision has been made by the Brussels Convention for the service of documents on European defendants covered by the Convention; a summons intended to be served under these provisions requires a special endorsement. This procedure is quite frequently employed because a significant number of libel actions are against foreign, usually English, defendants without an office in Ireland.

A summons can also be issued here for service out of the jurisdiction to countries not covered by the Convention. This requires an order of the court.

Defence

The defence is the defendant's principal document; in which he answers the plaintiff's statement of claim and denies any fact on the statement of claim which he or it intends to dispute: matters not denied will be taken to be admitted. The defence must contain one or more of the recognised defences to a libel action: justification, fair comment on a matter of public interest, privilege, no defamatory meaning and so on. It is perfectly possible to plead any and all defences in the alternative. Furthermore, they can be pleaded in the alternative so that the fact that one fails does not prejudice another. The defences must be pleaded in legally recognised form. Thus, for instance, the usual form of a plea of justification is that "the words complained of are true in substance and in fact". If it is desired to plead fair comment, the proper form is:

> "the words complained of in so far as consist of statements of fact, are true in substance and in fact and in so far as they consist of comment are fair comment made without malice on a matter of public interest."

It is important to note that the plea of fair comment, if it stands alone, will not be construed as including a plea of justification, which must be separately pleaded.[4]

Very frequently, a defence is filed merely as a holding measure, without any serious thought about whether there is a defence and if so what it is. It is always unwise to put in a defence merely as a holding device. Such defence will have to plead all possible defences. It can be highly prejudicial, particularly, to plead justification and then be forced to abandon it. The plaintiff will usually have identified the true meanings which he says attach to the publication of same on his statement of claim. The defendant would usually deny "that the words complained of bore, or were capable of bearing the meaning set out at paragraph X on the statement of claim, or any meaning defamatory of the plaintiff".

This is a very proper pleading if it is in fact intended to dispute all of the meanings alleged. But there is a great need for the defendant to be realistic: he should admit any meanings which the words plainly bear and, if appropriate, plead another defence such as justification in respect of them. For example, if the article alleged that the plaintiff had engaged in shop lifting, it would be unrealistic to deny that the words meant that the plaintiff had committed a criminal offence and was dishonest. Those meanings would have to be defended by a plea of justification or possibly privilege, or not at all. But it might be entirely reasonable to deny that the words meant that he was unfit for his occupation as a school teacher or some other extended meaning.

---

[4] *Burke v. Central Independent Television plc* [1994] 2 I.R. 61.

In general, a defendant who is contemplating denying any particular meaning should ask himself whether he will be quite comfortable standing over the denial in evidence. Or, on the contrary, would the denial put him into an artificial position, undermining his credibility with a court or jury?

Reply

Depending on the nature of the defence, the plaintiff may wish to deliver a rejoinder to it, known as a Reply. Especially where malice is denied, or privilege pleaded, this may be necessary. In the first case the rejoinder is necessary to make it perfectly clear that express malice is being contended for by the plaintiff. Where privilege is pleaded, the plaintiff will require to put on the record the factual basis of which he says that the occasion was not one of privilege or that the privilege has been lost, *e.g.* by excessive publication.

Particulars

It is open to either party to seek "further and better particulars" of the plaintiff's claim or of the defendant's defence. This is usually done first by the defendant after receipt of the statement of claim and later by the plaintiff after receipt of the defendant's defence. The particulars relate to the *nature* of the claim or defence: neither party is entitled to particulars of the *evidence* which its opponent proposes to need.

Particulars can be of great importance in libel cases. Ideally, they should bring about a situation in which neither party will be surprised by the nature of the case made by the other at the trial.

Particulars consist of a series of questions about the claim or defence which are first asked by letter. If there is no reply or only an unsatisfactory reply, proper answers can be compelled by motion to the court.

Of particular importance is the plaintiff's right to raise particulars of a defendant's plea of justification of fair comment. Following the case of *Cooney v. Browne*,[5] it has been established that the plaintiff is entitled, when these matters are pleaded, to a knowledge of "the

---

[5] [1985] I.R. 185.

full factual range" of the defence. Thus, he is entitled (a) to ask the defendant to state what portion of the words complained of is alleged to be fact and what portion is comment and (b) in relation to the facts, he is entitled to particulars of the facts which the defendant proposes to prove in order to establish the truth of the factual components of the words.

On the other hand, the defendant is entitled to rely on the statutory provision relating to partial justification, and is not obliged to give particulars in advance of what portions of the article or programme he suspects he will not be able to prove to be true. Where the plaintiff pleads actual damage, the defendant is entitled to full and detailed particulars of such damage.

Where innuendo is pleaded the defendant is entitled (if not already detailed in the statement of claim) to particulars of the extrinsic facts as a result of which the plaintiff claims that some or all of the defamatory meanings arise. Again, where the plaintiff is not identified by name, he is entitled to particulars of the extrinsic facts on the basis of which he claims some or all of the persons to whom the article is published would identify him.

A reading of the English textbooks on libel and procedure indicate a practice in the U.K., especially relating to particulars, which is somewhat stricter than that obtaining here. However, the trend of decisions here shows a tendency to approach the English level of strictness. A party is well advised will give particulars which are as complete as possible. However, if it is felt that the other side's particulars are sparse, and that this may put them at some disadvantage at trial, it is prudent to write to them significantly in advance of the hearing requesting further and better particulars and stating that an omission to provide these will be relied upon at the trial, as the basis of objection to evidence of the relevant kind.

Discovery

Discovery is a procedure whereby either party can compel the other to provide a list, authenticated by a sworn affidavit, of all documents in its "possession, power or procurement" which are relevant to the matters at issue in the proceedings. The scope of discovery extends to documents which were in the possession etc of a party but which he has since lost possession of.

The procedure envisages that the party from whom discovery is sought will make a list of all such documents authenticated on oath. The list will divide the documents into a number of categories, most relevantly those which he is prepared to disclose or produce, and those in respect of which he claims privilege. The idea of this is to give a full picture of the documents available so that the other party can, if so advised, challenge the claim of privilege.

In certain cases, documents can be of very great importance. For example, if an article accuses the plaintiff of financial impropriety in relation to some transaction, the obtaining of the documents in relation to it may put the defendant in a much stronger position to prove a plea of justification. Equally, discovery of the documents in the possession of a defendant may indicate to a plaintiff that the article complained of was not properly researched or that the defendant is likely to be in a very weak position from the point of view of proving a particular allegation. On the other hand, it may of course, indicate that the defendant has an unanswerable defence.

Generally, however, the object of discovery is simply to gain further information about the other side's case and to avoid surprise.

It is important to note that the fact that documents have been disclosed on discovery does not prove them. They must be proved, *i.e.* established to be authentic in the ordinary way. Furthermore, the disclosure of documents on discovery does not, of course, prove the truth of the contents of the document. Thus if a defendant obtains on discovery a letter from a third party setting out various facts which are favourable to the defendant, he must still set about proving these facts in the ordinary way. However, the fact that he has obtained the letter may very well put him in a much better position to do so, *e.g.* by summoning the writer to give evidence.

The question of privilege is a technical one which is best resolved before the trial. This can be done by bringing a motion to inspect the document. At the hearing of this motion, the claim of privilege will be fully debated. Experience suggests that media defendants often accept a plea of privilege too easily. The most common heading of privilege is legal professional privilege. However, not every document passing between a party and his solicitor is privileged; only material submitted for the purpose of obtaining legal advice comes into this category. In particular, instructions to perform some purely administrative act such as forming a company will not be privileged.

On the other hand once proceedings have commenced it is

overwhelmingly likely that the documents passing between a party and his solicitor are indeed privileged. This privilege will extend also to his solicitors who worked in preparing the case, *e.g.* the instruction of expert witnesses and their reports, witness statements, submissions to counsel and counsel's advice.

Discovery is normally obtainable only after the pleadings close. The effect of this is that a party must first set out his case and only then take procedures to gather evidence for it. There is power to order discovery at an earlier stage in exceptional circumstances. However, the general rule is that "fishing" applications for discovery are discouraged − this term indicates a situation where the plaintiff or defendant has no real idea what he is looking for and is applying for discovery simply in the hope that something unfavourable to the other party will turn up.

Notice to Admit and Interrogatories

It is open to a party to set out certain factual propositions and invite the other side to agree that they are true. This is done by a notice to admit facts and its purpose is to save time and costs at the trial. Thus, for example, a party who has obtained a very large bulk of documents may call on the other party to admit that the documents are authentic.

A party is never bound to make such an admission. If he does not the only sanction is that his opponent may fix him with the costs of proving the matters whose admission was sought, regardless of the outcome of the trial as a whole.

Sometimes, however, a party will find it difficult to plan the presentation of this case at trial unless he knows precisely what he can and cannot prove in advance. In these circumstances he may ask the court to permit him to deliver "interrogatories" to the other side. These are a series of questions generally of a sort that can be answered yes or no. A common instance of their employment is where a party to a road traffic accident suffers amnesia after the accident and lacks other witnesses. In these circumstances he may ask the other party such basic questions as whether he was driving a particular car, whether it was involved in an accident at a particular time and so on.

Since the recent case of *Mercantile Credit Company v. Heelan and others*[6] a number of points have been established in relation to interrogatories. The first is that something exceptional must be shown before they can be administered: the general rule is that trials proceed on oral evidence. Where something rather mechanical is the only matter at issue such as the admission of the authenticity of documents, interrogatories will usually be ordered. Interrogatories will not, however, be ordered as to the evidence in a party's possession. All applications for interrogatories, and indeed for discovery, must be shown to be relevant.

In the case of *Conlon v. Times Newspapers*, the defendant sought to interrogate the plaintiff on various topics including whether statements alleged to have been made by him to the English police, and set out in an official English report, were authentic. If this interrogatory had been answered in the affirmative it would of course have avoided the necessity to call the English police officers. In the event the interrogatories were disallowed on grounds of relevance following an appeal that is pending.

Third party discovery

Since the coming into force of the present Rules of the Superior Court in 1986, it has been possible for a party to proceedings to seek discovery against a person who is not a party. This procedure is more properly known as "non-party discovery" but the description above has gained acceptability.

This procedure provides a weapon of far reaching scope. It allows a party who can show that it is *likely* that a person or company who is not itself a party to the action nevertheless has documents in its possession, power or procurement which are relevant to the matters at issue. Once this is shown, an order can be granted against the non-party ordering discovery. The party seeking such discovery must pay the third party's costs and expenses immediately, and such sums then become part of his costs in the action.

In *Holloway v. Belenos Publications*[7] the former secretary of the Department of Energy, Mr Holloway, was suing the proprietors of *Business and Finance* arising from an article which the latter had

---

[6] *Irish Times Law Reports*, May 8, 1995.
[7] [1988] I.R. 494.

published relating to the Bula/Tara Mines saga. The article, he claimed, defamed him in relation to his discharge of his functions as secretary.

The defendant sought third party discovery against the minister himself seeking discovery of documents relevant to the matters at issue. This was at first refused on the basis that it had not been shown the Department were likely to have such documents. On re-application on somewhat changed facts, the Department sought to make the far-reaching claim that the rule permitting third party discovery was invalid and *ultra vires* (beyond the power of) the rule-making authority. This contention was rejected. The State appealed to the Supreme Court but withdrew the appeal on the day of the hearing. The action was subsequently settled.

It will be seen that scope of these various applications, notably for discovery and third party discovery, is very broad and can be of great assistance to a party and particularly, perhaps, to a defendant. However, the whole area of discovery in particular is highly technical and often raises difficult legal and tactical issues. It is essential to take advice in the context of the facts of any particular case.

Injunctions

An injunction is an order of the court directing the defendant to do or (more commonly) to refrain from doing a particular thing. Injunctions may be granted after a full hearing in which case they are usually "perpetual". More commonly, they are granted shortly after proceedings are commenced for the purpose of preserving the position until the full hearing can take place. The injunctions are known as "interlocutory". Finally, an injunction may sometimes be granted for a very short period, in order to preserve the posistion that the defendant can be heard on the question of whether there should be an interlocutory injunction. These injunctions are applied for *ex parte* (in the absence of the other side) and are referred to as "interim" injunctions.

A plaintiff who has successfully established that he has been libelled, and who has been awarded damages; will usually get a perpetual injunction restraining repetition of the libel for the asking. In fact, such injunctions are rarely sought because there is seldom any reason to believe that a media defendant will repeat something which has been conclusively proved to be an indefensible libel.

Perpetual injunctions in these circumstances are common where the defendant is an individial.

The area of interim interlocutory injunctions is of more practical interest. If a person learns in advance that it is intended to publish something defamatory of him, it is much more useful for him to prevent the publication taking place at all than to sue for damages after the event. Alternatively, where the libel is contained in a book or magazine he may see it shortly after publication and think of trying to prevent further sales.

The court undoubtedly has power to grant an injunction restraining the publication or the republication of a libel.[8] Prior to that case there has been considerable doubt as to the terms of which such an injunction would be granted, and even as to whether there was a power to grant an injunction restraining a publication. Although this power is now established, the conditions for its exercise in cases of alleged libel are different and much more onerous on a plaintiff, than those applying in the case of any other civil wrong.

A person applying for an injunction to restrain publication of a libel must show:

1. A *prima facie* case of libel,

2. Evidence that the defendant is likely to publish the libel, or publish it further than has already been done and,

3. that such publication will inflict on the plaintiff an injury which cannot be fully compensated in damages.

Even when these matters have been established, the court has a considerable discretion. In *Sinclair v. Gogarty* (above), it was observed that the jurisdiction was "of a delicate nature". In practice a pre-trial injunction will not be granted if *either* there is any doubt that the words are defamatory *or* if the defendant swears that he intends to plead justification or any other recognised defence, unless such defence is plainly unstateable. In other words, the plaintiff has to show, at a very early stage, that it is most unlikely that the defendant will succeed.

The reason for these unusually onerous requirements is that the injunction restraining the publication of a libel involves

---

[8] *Sinclair v. Gogarty* [1937] I.R. 377.

interfering with the defendant's constitutional right to freedom of expression.

The result of this approach on the part of the courts has been that very few applications for interlocutory injunctions restraining publication of libel have been made, and fewer still have succeeded. The rationale underlining the courts attitude was well set out in the judgment of Carroll J. in *Attorney General for England and Wales v. Brandon Books*.[9] This was not a libel case but an application to restrain publication of a book by a lady who had been employed in the British Secret Service many years before. The book, it was alleged, represented a breach of her obligation of confidentiality. Carroll J. refused to grant the injunction, relying on the dfendant's constitutional right to publish and pointing out that it was a right to publish "immediately", and not at some unascertained future date after the case had been disposed of. This attitude also underlies the judicial approach to libel injunctions.

Nevertheless injunctions have been given in suitable cases. *Sinclair v. Gogarty* was one such situation, where, it turned out, there was a real attempt at justification. The defendant contended himself by contending that the plaintiffs were not identified, and that the words were not defamatory. The High Court and Supreme Court each took the view that the words were beyond argument defamatory and there was ample evidence that they referred to the plaintiff. In these circumstances the injunction was granted. It may be that the attitude of the court was influenced by the fact that the libel was regarded as a particularly foul one.

Injunctions were also granted in the case of *Trainor v. Independent Newspapers*.[10] This was a most unusual case in that the plaintiff sought an injunction on the basis that he had been told by a journalist writing for the defendant that she was going to publish a story about him which she acknowledged to be false. Some two weeks after the initial application came out, the journalist in question was shot and died without having put in an affidavit. No other affidavit was filed on behalf of the defendant. The allegations proposed to be published were of a very serious nature. In these circumstances the court granted an injunction.

It is of course usual for a plaintiff to have any information in

---

[9] [1988] I.R. 597.
[10] Unreported, High Court, Barron J., 1996).

advance that a defamation is about to be published of him by a newspaper. The development of investigative journalism naming the plaintiffs will have this information more frequently because the investigation itself may come to their attention through requests for interviews or otherwise. Accordingly, this is an area of the law which may develop in the near future in particular, the present practice whereby a defendant is merely required to indicate on oath that he will defend the action (as opposed to showing any evidence showing a defence) will be reviewed.

10. COPYRIGHT AND DATA PROTECTION

Copyright allows people to benefit from their own original work in the knowledge that it will not be pirated or exploited by others. It gives a right to prevent copying. The law here is contained in the Copyright Act of 1963 which came into force on October 10, 1964. It has been amended by the European Communities (Term of Protection of Copyright) Regulations 1995 and a new Copyright Act is expected to be implemented shortly. What works are protected?

Basically the Act covers a range of works that are entitled to copyright protection. They are: (a) literary works; (b) dramatic works; (c) musical works; (d) artistic works; (e) sound recordings; (f) cinematograph films; (g) broadcasts; (h) published editions of works; (i) Irish legal tender. The English equivalent is the Copyright Designs and Patents Act of 1988.

Literary works

The most important area of copyright from a journalist's point of view is undoubtedly that provided to literary works.

Included in this category are books, newspaper reports, computer programmes and in Ireland the written report of a speech. Published works are protected until the end of the 70th year after the author's death. In the case of unpublished works which are posthumously published copyright will expire after a period of six years from the end of the year in which the publication takes place.

Section 8(VI) sets out the acts restricted by the copyright in a literary, dramatic or musical work and/or (a) reproducing the work in any material form; (b) publishing the work; (c) performing the work in public; (d) broadcasting the work; (e) causing the work to be transmitted to subscribers to a diffusion service; (f) making any adaptation of the work; (g) doing, in relation to an adaptation of the work, any of the acts mentioned in paragraphs (a) to (e) of this subsection.

Ownership of the copyright

Generally speaking, the author of an original literary, dramatic musical or artistic work is entitled to the copyright subsisting in that work. Where a work is made by the author in the course of his or her employment, an employer is the first owner of the copyright unless there is an agreement to the contrary. From a practical point of view a staff journalist who creates a literary, dramatic or artistic work in the course of his or her employment for the proprietor of a newspaper magazine or similar periodical then the proprietor should be entitled to the copyright in the work. This only relates to the publication of the work in a newspaper, magazine or similar periodical or to its reproduction for the purpose of its being published but in all other respects the author should be entitled to the copyright.

Sound recording and broadcasts

For journalists working in these areas television broadcasts are subject to copyright protection for 70 years. A period of 50 years applies in the case of sound recordings from the end of the year in which they are made. The acts restricted by the copyright in a television broadcast or a sound broadcast are:

(a) in the case of a visual broadcast insofar as it consists of visual images, making, otherwise than for private purposes a cinematograph film of it or part of it or a photograph of part of it or a copy of such film or photograph.

(b) in the case of a sound broadcast or a television broadcast insofar as it consists of sounds made otherwise than for private purposes a sound recording of it or a recording embodying such a recording.

(c) in the case of a television broadcast causing it insofar as it consists of visual images to be seen in public or insofar as it consists of sounds to be heard in public if it is seen or heard by a paying audience.

(d) in the case either of a television broadcast or of a sound broadcast, re-broadcasting it.

Protecting the copyright

Ironically enough, Ireland requires no formalities for the protection of the copyright. Many people think that the 'C' surrounded by a circle is essential to establishing copyright but this is not the case. However, it is always advisable to use it if you are establishing a copyright. It is important to remember that there is no monopoly in relation to copyright if two independent people publish work at the same time when each would be entitled to the copyright in that work.

Defences to infringement of copyright

The main defences in relation to an infringement of copyright would be to allege fair dealing or to claim that it was in the public interest such as reproducing something for a court proceeding or the infringement resulted from practical considerations. If a copyright owner can prove that his copyright has been infringed he can apply to the courts for an injunction and he will also be entitled to seek damages from the person infringing his copyright. An Irish case in the area of copyright is *R.T.É. v. Magill T.V. Guide Ltd* .[1] This decision which went against *Magill* was appealed to the European Court where *Magill* were the successful parties.

Broadcasting

Broadcasters in both radio and television have to be particularly careful applying the law relating to defamation and contempt. Inevitably, material on occasions can be exposed to a wider audience than that of a newspaper. Television broadcasters have to be particularly careful when editing material to make sure that the script and the pictures accompanying it are both free of defamatory material and are not contemptuous. Editing of material for television must be done with great care particularly if there is criticism of individuals or other businesses involved.

---

[1] [1988] I.R. 97.

Live broadcasts

There is a popular misconception in regard to live broadcasts that the broadcasting authority will not be held liable for defamatory material broadcast by an individual invited onto a programme. Live programmes don't enjoy any special legal protection whatsoever. Not only can the broadcasting authority and its employees be sued but also the person making the defamatory comment, although in some instances the broadcasting authority may well decide to defend not only on its own behalf but on behalf of the contributing individual.

Controlling broadcasting

The 1960 Broadcasting Acts saw the establishment of R.T.É., a semi-State body to oversee the development of television and sound in the State. R.T.É. was given a monopoly over such services and was financed by the State but was allowed to advertise. The Act also imposed the requirements of fairness and impartiality, regard for privacy and, more controversially, gave the Minister the right to direct the authority to refrain from broadcasting certain matters.[2] As with all semi-State bodies at that time the Minister had the power to appoint the authority. While the Broadcasting Act was amended in 1976, the real wind of change came in the late 1980's with the establishment of the Radio and Television Act of 1988 which provided for the establishment of the I.R.T.C. (The Independent Radio and Television Commission). It had the power to issue licences and while we have not seen as yet the establishment of a completely independent television station, many regions are now enjoying an alternative to R.T.É. Radio with the establishment of independent radio stations. Like R.T.É., the requirements of impartial reporting and the requirement with regard to privacy is imposed by the Act.

Like the R.T.É. authority, the Independent Radio and Television Commission is a body appointed by the government. An attempt to cap advertising revenue to R.T.É. was not successful and latest audience figures show that the independent radio stations particularly in the Dublin area are holding their own against R.T.É.

---

[2] Section 31.

Court challenges

In recent times the I.R.T.C. has had proceedings taken against it by Radio Limerick for failing to grant it a licence. Although successful that case is now under appeal to the Supreme Court.[3] In the eighties the monopoly position of R.T.É. was challenged by two companies in the cases of *Nova Media services Ltd v. Minister for Posts and Telegraphs*[4] and *Sunshine Radio v. Minister for Posts and Telegraphs*.[5] Both challenges were unsuccessful.

Broadcasting Complaints Commission

The Broadcasting Complaints Commission which was set up under the Broadcasting Authority (amendment) Act of 1976 considers complaints both against the R.T.É. authority and the I.R.T.C. The jurisdiction of the commission is strictly confined to investigating and deciding limited classes of complaints. They are (a) news; (b) current affairs; (c) ministerial prohibitions; (d) invasion of privacy; (e) advertising. Unlike Britain, we do not have a Broadcasting Standards Council. It is important to note that our Broadcasting Commission cannot impose any sanctions, it merely produces a report into the complaint. Membership of the Commission consists of a minimum of three people appointed by the government who act in a part-time capacity.

Official Secrets

1963 saw the enactment not only of the Copyright Act but also of the Official Secrets Act. Section 4 provides that a person shall not communicate any official information to any other person unless he is duly authorised to do so or does so in the course of and in accordance with his duty as a holder of a public office or when it is his duty in the interests of the State to communicate it. A person to whom this applies shall take reasonable care to avoid any unlawful communication of such information.

---

[3] *Madden v. The I.R.T.C.*, unreported, High Court, October, 1996.
[4] [1984] I.L.R.M. 161.
[5] [1984] I.L.R.M. 170.

A Journalist's Point of View

Section 6 states that a person shall not retain any official document or anything which constitutes or contains official information when he has no right to retain it or when not required by his duty as the holder of a public office to retain it. It is this section that could get a journalist into trouble and provision is made in the Act for the prosecution of any person who contravenes or attempts to contravene any provision of the Act. In addition there is provision for holding such proceedings in camera if the prosecution can show that the material would be prejudicial to the safety or preservation of the State. In such a case the verdict and sentence has to be announced in public.

In practical terms the Official Secrets Act has not created much trouble to date for journalists but it is an outdated Act and is probably in need of review. One interesting case was brought against Brandon Book Publishers Ltd. when the Attorney General for England and Wales came to court seeking to restrain the publication of a book written by a deceased member of the British Secret Service on the grounds of confidentiality claimed from the employment of the authoress.[6] Brandon countered by claiming a right to publish the book by virtue of Article 46(1) of the Constitution which guarantees the liberties of the exercise of the right of the citizens to freely express convictions and opinions subject to public order and morality. The Attorney General for England and Wales was unsuccessful and it is interesting to note that Ms Justice Carroll laid great emphasis on the judgment of Mason J. in *Fairfax & Sons Ltd*[7] where he stated:

> ". . . The equitable principle has been fashioned to protect the personal, private and proprietary rights of the citizen, not to protect the very different interests of the executive government. It acts, or is supposed to act, not according to standards of private interest, but in the public interest. This is not to say that equity will not protect information in the hands of the government, but it is to say that when equity protects government information it will look at the matter through

---

[6] *Attorney General for England and Wales v. Brandon Books Publishers* [1987] I.L.R.M. 135.
[7] (1980) 147 C.L.R. 39.

different spectacles. It may be a sufficient detriment to the citizen that disclosure of information relating to his affairs will expose his actions to public discussion and criticism. But it can scarcely be a relevant detriment to the government that publication of material concerning its actions will merely expose it to public discussion and criticism. It is unacceptable in our democratic society that there should be a restraint on the publication of information relating to government when the only vice of that information is that it enables the public to discuss, review and criticise government action. Accordingly, the Court will determine the government's claim to confidentiality by reference to the public interest. Unless disclosure is likely to injure the public interest, it will not be protected."

Viewed as a statement of the law, it provides a good guide for journalists who may have a query in regard to this whole area of official secrets and breach of confidentiality.

The Data Protection Act

The Data Protection Act of 1988 gives effect to the Convention for the protection of individuals with regard to automatic processing of personal data. By personal data is meant information recorded on a computer about living, identifiable individuals. A subject is an individual to whom personal data relates and data users are people or organisations who control the contents and use or collection of personal data. Generally speaking it would be a company or other organisation but it is possible in this electronic age for an individual to be a data user. The purpose of the Act is to give limited protection in respect of certain types of data being held in an electronic form. Sections 1 to 8 of the Data Protection Act 1988, in relation to the collection, processing, keeping and disclosure of personal data, are included in Appendix 2.

Section 2 of the Act provides that a data controller shall in respect of personal data kept by him comply with the following provisions:

1. The data or as the case may be the information constituting the data shall have been obtained, and the data should be processed, fairly.

2. The data shall be accurate and where necessary kept up to date.

3. The data shall be kept for one or more specified and lawful purposes and shall not be used or disclosed in any manner incompatible with that purpose or those purposes.

4. It shall be adequate, relevant and not excessive in relation to that purpose or those purposes and shall not be kept for longer than is necessary for that purpose or those purposes.

There is also a requirement that appropriate security measures should be taken against unauthorised access to or alteration, disclosure or destruction of the data and against the accidental loss or destruction.

An individual is entitled to be informed by any data user whether he has personal data of which that individual is the subject and has the right of access to such data.

There are also provisions in relation to the right of access and they are covered in section 4. Section 5 deals with the restrictions on the right of access.

The Data Protection Commissioner may investigate whether any of the provisions of this Act have been or are being or are likely to be contravened by a Data Controller or a Data Processor in relation to an individual either where the individual complains to him of a contravention or any of those provisions or he is otherwise of the opinion that there may be such a contravention.

Advertising

Advertising plays an important role in any media operation and although it is only being referred to very briefly in this book the importance of its role cannot be overemphasised.

Advertising Standards Authority

There are a wide range of regulations and items of legislation dealing with all aspects of advertising and a journalist in doubt should contact the Advertising Standards Authority for Ireland (ASAI) which is a self-regulating body established by the industry in 1981. The ASAI will investigate complaints from members of the public relating to a particular advertisement and issue a finding on the matter and while its decisions are not legally binding, it has a very good reputation within the advertising industry and would certainly guide a journalist in the correct direction in relation to the minefield of regulations that need to be adhered to in this area. They have issued a comprehensive code to its members and copies can be obtained by contacting the ASAI. Both RTE and the Independent Radio and Television Commission also quote standards and again the Broadcasting Complaints Commission will hear any complaint which is in breach of the Code of Standards.

Furthermore, it must be borne in mind that the consumer is protected under the Consumer Information Act of 1978 against misleading advertising. Again, the impact of the Act is enforced by the Director of Consumer Affairs who can take action against advertisers who are misleading or unfair.

On a European level the practice of comparative advertising is being dealt with by means of the implementation of a directive on the matter. Currently being discussed, the aim of the directive is to harmonise the laws of Member States on comparative advertising and one effect could be that both indirect and direct advertising will be allowed in all Member States.

APPENDIX 1

THE HIGH COURT

BETWEEN:

JOHN SMITH   [Title]

Plaintiff

– and –

MICHAEL MILITANT

AND

DAILY SCREAM LTD

Defendants

GENERAL ENDORSEMENT OF CLAIM

[Brief
statement of
the general
nature of the
plaintiff's
claim]

The plaintiff's claim is for

(a) Damages for libel

(b) An injunction restraining the defendants and each of them, their servants or agents, and any person having notice of the making of an Order of this Honourable Court, from publishing of and concerning the plaintiff the words set out in the Schedule to the Statement of Claim in this action or any words to the same effect.

(c) Further or other relief.

(d) Costs.

[Signature of
plaintiff's
counsel]

E. Morse, S.C.
E. Holmes, B.L.

(1) This Honourable Court has power to hear and determine the claim referred to in these proceedings pursuant to the provisions of the Jurisdiction of Courts and Enforcement of Judgments (European Communities) Act 1988 and pursuant to Article 1 and Article 5.3 of the Convention on Jurisdiction and the Enforcement of Judgments in Civil and Commercial Matters signed in Brussels on September 27, 1968.

(2) There are no other proceedings concerning the same cause of action pending between the parties to these proceedings before the courts of any other contracting State to which the 1968 Convention applies

Signed: ....

THE HIGH COURT

BETWEEN

JOHN SMITH

Plaintiff

– and –

MICHAEL MILITANT

AND

DAILY SCREAM LTD

Defendants

STATEMENT OF CLAIM

Delivered this 1st day of April 1997 by Patrick Murphy solicitor for the plaintiff.

[indication of status of each defendant and their addresses].

1. The plaintiff is a schoolteacher and resides at 25, Happy Valley, Dublin 31.

2. The first named defendant is a freelance journalist and resides at 34, Grubb St., Dublin 1. The second named defendant is a Limited Liability Company incorporated in the United Kingdom of Great Britain and Northern Ireland and carries on business at 17 Yellow Press Road London WC 1.

[allegation of publication in Ireland]

3. The second named defendant is a newspaper publisher and publishes amongst other titles the Daily Scream, which is a tabloid newspaper of wide circulation. The said newspaper is printed in the United Kingdom and distributed, *inter alia*, within the jurisdiction of this Honourable Court.

[allegation of reference to the plaintiff and of falsity and malice]

4. On or about the 20th day of March 1997, the first named defendant wrote, for publication by the second named defendant, the words set out in the First Schedule hereto. The second named defendant published the said words and distributed them, *inter alia*, within the jurisdiction of this Honourable Court.

5. The said words were so written and published by the defendants falsely and maliciously of and concerning the plaintiff.

[allegation of defamatory nature of the words and indication that innuendo is relied on]

6. The said words in their ordinary and natural meaning, further or in the alternative by innuendo, are grossly defamatory of the plaintiff and have damaged him in his character and reputation and exposed him to odium, ridicule and contempt.

7. The said words in their ordinary and natural meaning, further or in the alternative by innuendo, meant and were understood to mean:

[meanings alleged, by innuendo or otherwise]

   (a) that the plaintiff is a drug-dealer, that is one who deals in prohibited drugs for reward;

   (b) further or in the alternative that the plaintiff is with reasonable cause suspected of being a drug dealer;

   (c) that the plaintiff has committed and continues to commit serious criminal offences;

   (d) that the plaintiff is unfit to be retained in his employment as a school-teacher and is unfit to hold his elected office as a County Councillor;

   (e) that the plaintiff has betrayed the trust reposed in him in both of the aforesaid capacities;

   (f) that the plaintiff is a hypocrite;

   (g) that the plaintiff is unfit for the society of law-abiding people.

[particulars of express malice]

8. PARTICULARS OF FACTS, EXTRINSIC TO THE WORDS COMPLAINED OF, RELIED UPON TO GROUND THE INNUENDO MEANINGS

The plaintiff is a registered teacher at St. Elsewhere's school. He has pastoral responsibility for a class of pupils there. He is an elected member of the County Council. In that capacity he has been an active vocal campaigner against drug use and in particular the supply of drugs to young people.

9. The words complained of were published with express malice towards the plaintiff on the part of the defendants and each of them.

10. PARTICULARS OF MALICE

The defendants published the words in question knowing them to have been false or alternatively reckless as to whether they were true or false. They made no attempt to contact the plaintiff prior to publishing them or to afford him any opportunity to rebut or comment on them. In so doing they were motivated by a desire to increase the circulation of the Daily Scream by publishing a sensational story and by a desire to destroy the plaintiff's political career.

AND the plaintiff claims:

(a) Damages for libel.

(b) An injunction restraining the defendants and each of them their servants or agents or any person having notice of the Order of this Honourable Court from repeating or re-publishing in any form whatsoever the words set out in the Schedule hereto or any words to the same effect.

(c) Further or other relief.

(d) costs.

E. Morse S.C.
S. Holmes, B.L.

SCHEDULE

NET CLOSES ON DRUGS' MR. BIG

The Daily Scream has learnt that an arrest is imminent in the hunt for Dublin's drug czar. While no name is mentioned officially, well-placed sources are increasingly interested in John Smith, the outspoken anti-drugs campaigner who, they suggest, has been leading a double life. An official spokeman refused to confirm or deny that Smith (53) is the prime target.

(the said words were accompanied by a photograph of the plaintiff with a caption "Smith: double life?")

THE HIGH COURT

BETWEEN

JOHN SMITH
Plaintiff

– and –

MICHAEL MILITANT

AND

DAILY SCREAM LTD
Defendants

DEFENCE

Delivered the 4th day of June 1997 by Jones Green White Associates, solicitors for the defendants.

[or any meaning defamatory of the plaintiff]

1. Paragraphs 1 and 2 of the Statement of Claim herein are admitted.

2. The words complained of, in their ordinary and natural meaning or by innuendo, do not bear the meanings set out in the Statement of Claim and are not defamatory.

[plea of justification]

3. The said words in their true meaning, and without the special meanings pleaded, are true in substance and in fact.

[plea of fair comment]

4. Insofar as the said words consists of statements of fact, they are true and accurate; insofar as they consist of comment they are fair comment made without malice on a matter of public interest, to wit the progress of official enquiries into serious crime.

[denial of damage]

5. The plaintiff has not been damaged in his character or reputation or exposed to odium ridicule or contempt as alleged or at all.

6. The plaintiff is not entitled to the relief claimed or to any relief.

H. Poirot, S.C.
J. Marples, B.L.

APPENDIX 2

DEFAMATION ACT, 1961 (NUMBER 40 OF 1961)

PART I
Preliminary and General

1.—This Act may be cited as the Defamation Act, 1961.

2.—In this Act—

"local authority" has the same meaning as in the Local Government Act, 1941;

"newspaper", except in section 27, means any paper containing public news or observations thereon, or consisting wholly or mainly of advertisements, which is printed for sale and is published in the State or in Northern Ireland either periodically or in parts or numbers at intervals not exceeding thirty-six days;

"proprietor" means, as well as the sole proprietor of any newspaper, in the case of a divided proprietorship, the persons who, as partners or otherwise, represent or are responsible for any share or interest in the newspaper as between themselves and the persons in like manner representing or responsible for the other shares or interests therein, and no other person.

3.—(1) This Act shall come into operation on the 1st day of January, 1962.

(2) Part III of this Act shall apply for the purposes of any proceedings begun after the commencement of this Act, whenever the cause of action arose, but shall not affect any proceedings commenced before the commencement of this Act.

4.—The enactments specified in the First Schedule to this Act are hereby repealed.

Part II
Criminal Proceedings for Libel

5.—(1) On every trial of an indictment for making or publishing any libel to which a plea of not guilty is entered, the jury may give a general verdict of guilty or not guilty upon the whole matter put in issue on the indictment, and the jury shall not be required or directed by the court to find the person charged guilty merely on the proof of the publication by him of the paper charged to be a libel and of the sense ascribed to such paper in the indictment

(2) On every such trial the court shall, according to its discretion, give its opinion and directions to the jury on the matter in issue in like manner as in other criminal cases.

(3) Subsections (1) and *(2)* of this section shall not operate to prevent the jury from finding a special verdict, in their discretion, as in other criminal cases.

6.—On the trial of any indictment for a defamatory libel, the person charged having pleaded such plea as hereinafter mentioned, the truth of the matters charged may be inquired into but shall not amount to a defence, unless it was for the public benefit that the said matters charged should be published; and, to entitle the defendant to give evidence of the truth of such matters charged as a defence to such indictment, it shall be necessary for the person charged, in pleading to the said indictment, to allege the truth of the said matters charged, in the manner required in pleading a justification to an action for defamation, and further to allege that it was for the public benefit that the said matters charged should be published, and the particular fact or facts by reason of which it was for the public benefit that the said matters charged should be published, to which plea the prosecutor shall be at liberty to reply generally, denying the whole thereof; and if, after such plea, the person charged is convicted on such indictment, the court may, in pronouncing sentence, consider whether his guilt is aggravated or mitigated by the said plea and by the evidence given to prove or to disprove the same: provided that—

    (*a*) the truth of the matters charged in the alleged libel complained of by such indictment shall in no case be inquired into without such plea of justification;

    (*b*) in addition to such plea of justification, the person charged may enter a plea of not guilty;

(*c*) nothing in this section shall take away or prejudice any defence under the plea of not guilty which it is competent to the person charged to make under such plea to any indictment for defamatory libel.

7.—Whenever, upon the trial of an indictment for the publication of a libel, a plea of not guilty having been entered, evidence is given establishing a presumption of publication against the person charged by the act of any other person by his authority, it shall be competent for the person charged to prove that the publication was made without his authority, consent or knowledge and that the publication did not arise from want of due care or caution on his part.

8.—No criminal prosecution shall be commenced against any proprietor, publisher, editor or any person responsible for the publication of a newspaper for any libel published therein without the order of a Judge of the High Court sitting *in camera* being first had and obtained, and every application for such order shall be made on notice to the person accused, who shall have an opportunity of being heard against the application.

9.—A Justice of the District Court, upon the hearing of a charge against a proprietor, publisher or editor or any person responsible for the publication of a newspaper for a libel published therein, may receive evidence as to the publication being for the public benefit, as to the matters charged in the libel being true, as to the report being fair and accurate and published without malice and as to any matter which, under this or any other Act or otherwise, might be given in evidence by way of defence by the person charged on his trial on indictment, and the Justice, if of opinion after hearing such evidence that there is a strong or probable presumption that the jury on the trial would acquit the person charged, may dismiss the case.

10.—If a Justice of the District Court upon the hearing of a charge against a proprietor, publisher, editor or any person responsible for the publication of a newspaper for a libel published therein, is of opinion that, though the person charged is shown to have been guilty, the libel was of a trivial character and that the offence may be adequately punished by virtue of the powers conferred by this section, the Justice shall cause the charge to be reduced into writing and read to the person charged and shall then ask him if he desires to be tried by a jury or consents to the case being dealt with summarily, and, if such person consents to the case being dealt with summarily, may summarily convict him, and impose on him a fine not exceeding fifty pounds, and the Summary Jurisdiction Acts shall apply accordingly.

11.—Every person who maliciously publishes any defamatory libel shall, on conviction thereof on indictment, be liable to a fine not exceeding two hundred pounds or to imprisonment for a term not exceeding one year or to both such fine and imprisonment.

12.—Every person who maliciously publishes any defamatory libel, knowing the same to be false, shall, on conviction thereof on indictment, be liable to a fine not exceeding five hundred pounds or to imprisonment for a term not exceeding two years or to both such fine and imprisonment.

13.—(1) Every person who composes, prints or publishes any blasphemous or obscene libel shall, on conviction thereof on indictment, be liable to a fine not exceeding five hundred pounds or to imprisonment for a term not exceeding two years or to both such fine and imprisonment or to penal servitude for a term not exceeding seven years.

    (2)(*a*) In every case in which a person is convicted of composing, printing or publishing a blasphemous libel, the court may make an order for the seizure and carrying away and detaining in safe custody, in such manner as shall be directed in the order, of all copies of the libel in the possession of such person or of any other person named in the order for his use, evidence upon oath having been previously given to the satisfaction of the court that copies of the said libel are in the possession of such other person for the use of the person convicted;

      (*b*) Upon the making of an order under paragraph (a) of this subsection, any member of the Garda Síochána acting under such order may enter, if necessary by the use of force, and search for any copies of the said libel any building, house or other place belonging to the person convicted or to such other person named in the order and may seize and carry away and detain in the manner directed in such order all copies of the libel found therein;

(c) If, in any such case, the conviction is quashed on appeal, any copies of the libel seized under an order under paragraph (a) of this subsection shall be returned free of charge to the person or persons from whom they were seized;

(d) Where, in any such case, an appeal is not lodged or the conviction is confirmed on appeal, any copies of the libel seized under an order under paragraph (a) of this subsection shall, on the application of a member of the Garda Síochána to the court which made such order, be disposed of in such manner as such court may direct.

PART III
Civil Proceedings for Defamation

14.—(1) In this Part—

"broadcast" has the same meaning as in the Wireless Telegraphy Act, 1926 (in this section referred to as the Act of 1926) and "broadcasting" shall be construed accordingly;

"broadcasting station" has the same meaning as in the Act of 1926 as amended by the Broadcasting Authority Act, 1960;

"wireless telegraphy" has the same meaning as in the Act of 1926

(2) Any reference in this Part to words shall be construed as including a reference to visual images, gestures and other methods of signifying meaning.

(3) Where words broadcast by means of wireless telegraphy are simultaneously transmitted by telegraph as defined by the Telegraph Act, 1863, in accordance with a licence granted by the Minister for Posts and Telegraphs, the provisions of this Part shall apply as if the transmission were broadcasting by means of wireless telegraphy.

15.—For the purposes of the law of libel and slander the broadcasting of words by means of wireless telegraphy shall be treated as publication in permanent form.

16.—Words spoken and published which impute unchastity or adultery to any woman or girl shall not require special damage to render them actionable.

17.—In any action for defamation, it shall be lawful for the defendant (after notice in writing of his intention so to do, duly given to the plaintiff at the time of filing or delivering the plea in the action) to give in evidence, in mitigation of damage, that he made or offered an apology to the plaintiff for such defamation before the commencement of the action, or as soon afterwards as he had an opportunity of doing so, in case the action shall have been commenced before there was an opportunity of making or offering such apology.

18.—(1) A fair and accurate report published in any newspaper or broadcast by means of wireless telegraphy as part of any programme or service provided by means of a broadcasting station within the State or in Northern Ireland of proceedings publicly heard before any court established by law and exercising judicial authority within the State or in Northern Ireland shall, if published or broadcast contemporaneously with such proceedings, be privileged.

(2) Nothing in subsection (1) of this section shall authorise the publication or broadcasting of any blasphemous or obscene matter.

19.—In an action for slander in respect of words calculated to disparage the plaintiff in any office, profession, calling, trade or business held or carried on by him at the time of the publication, it shall not be necessary to allege or prove special damage, whether or not the words are spoken of the plaintiff in the way of his office, profession, calling, trade or business.

20.—(1) In an action for slander of title, slander of goods or other malicious falsehood, it shall not be necessary to allege or prove special damage—

    (*a*) if the words upon which the action is founded are calculated to cause pecuniary damage to the plaintiff and are published in writing or other permanent form; or

    (*b*) if the said words are calculated to cause pecuniary damage to the plaintiff in respect of any office, profession, calling, trade or business held or carried on by him at the time of the publication.

(2) Section 15 of this Act shall apply for the purposes of subsection (1) of this section as it applies for the purposes of the law of libel and slander.

21.—(1) A person who has published words alleged to be defamatory of another person may, if he claims that the words were published by him innocently in relation to that other person, make an offer of amends under this section, and in any such case—

(*a*) if the offer is accepted by the party aggrieved and is duly performed, no proceedings for libel or slander shall be taken or continued by that party against the person making the offer in respect of the publication in question (but without prejudice to any cause of action against any other person jointly responsible for that publication);

(*b*) if the offer is not accepted by the party aggrieved, then, except as otherwise provided by this section, it shall be a defence, in any proceedings by him for libel or slander against the person making the offer in respect of the publication in question, to prove that the words complained of were published by the defendant innocently in relation to the plaintiff and that the offer was made as soon as practicable after the defendant received notice that they were or might be defamatory of the plaintiff, and has not been withdrawn.

(2) An offer of amends under this section must be expressed to be made for the purposes of this section, and must be accompanied by an affidavit specifying the facts relied upon by the person making it to show that the words in question were published by him innocently in relation to the party aggrieved and for the purposes of a defence under paragraph (b) of subsection (1) of this section no evidence, other than evidence of facts specified in the affidavit, shall be admissible on behalf of that person to prove that the words were so published.

(3) An offer of amends under this section shall be understood to mean an offer—

(*a*) in any case, to publish or join in the publication of a suitable correction of the words complained of, and a sufficient apology to the party aggrieved in respect of those words;

(*b*) where copies of a document or record containing the said words have been distributed by or with the knowledge of the person making the offer, to take such steps as are reasonably practicable on his part for notifying persons to whom copies have been so distributed that the words are alleged to be defamatory of the party aggrieved.

(4) Where an offer of amends under this section is accepted by the party aggrieved—

    (*a*) any question as to the steps to be taken in fulfilment of the offer as so accepted shall, in default of agreement between the parties, be referred to and determined by the High Court or, if proceedings in respect of the publication in question have been taken in the Circuit Court by the Circuit Court, and the decision of such Court thereon shall be final;

    (*b*) the power of the court to make orders as to costs in proceedings by the party aggrieved against the person making the offer in respect of the publication in question, or in proceedings in respect of the offer under paragraph (a) of this subsection, shall include power to order the payment by the person making the offer to the party aggrieved of costs on an indemnity basis and any expenses reasonably incurred or to be incurred by that party in consequence of the publication in question;

and if no such proceedings as aforesaid are taken, the High Court may, upon application made by the party aggrieved, make any such order for the payment of such costs and expenses as aforesaid as could be made in such proceedings.

(5) For the purposes of this section words shall be treated as published by one person (in this subsection referred to as the publisher) innocently in relation to another person if, and only if, the following conditions are satisfied, that is to say—

    (*a*) that the publisher did not intend to publish them of and concerning that other person, and did not know of circumstances by virtue of which they might be understood to refer to him; or

    (*b*) that the words were not defamatory on the face of them, and the publisher did not know of circumstances by virtue of which they might be understood to be defamatory of that other person, and in either case that the publisher exercised all reasonable care in relation to the publication; and any reference in this subsection to the publisher shall be construed as including a reference to any servant or agent of the publisher who was concerned with the contents of the publication.

(6) Paragraph (b) of subsection (1) of this section shall not apply

where the party aggrieved proves that he has suffered special damage.

(7) Paragraph (b) of subsection (1) of this section shall not apply in relation to the publication by any person of words of which he is not the author unless he proves that the words were written by the author without malice.

22.—In an action for libel or slander in respect of words containing two or more distinct charges against the plaintiff, a defence of justification shall not fail by reason only that the truth of every charge is not proved, if the words not proved to be true do not materially injure the plaintiff's reputation having regard to the truth of the remaining charges.

23.—In an action for libel or slander in respect of words consisting partly of allegations of fact and partly of expression of opinion, a defence of fair comment shall not fail by reason only that the truth of every allegation of fact is not proved, if the expression of opinion is fair comment having regard to such of the facts alleged or referred to in the words complained of as are proved.

24.—(1) Subject to the provisions of this section, the publication in a newspaper or the broadcasting by means of wireless telegraphy as part of any programme or service provided by means of a broadcasting station within the State or in Northern Ireland of any such report or other matter as is mentioned in the Second Schedule to this Act shall be privileged unless the publication or broadcasting is proved to be made with malice.

(2) In an action for libel in respect of the publication or broadcasting of any such report or matter as is mentioned in Part II of the Second Schedule to this Act, the provisions of this section shall not be a defence if it is proved that the defendant has been requested by the plaintiff to publish in the newspaper in which the original publication was made or to broadcast from the broadcasting station from which the original broadcast was made, whichever is the case, a reasonable statement by way of explanation or contradiction, and has refused or neglected to do so, or has done so in a manner not adequate or not reasonable having regard to all the circumstances.

(3) Nothing in this section shall be construed as protecting the publication or broadcasting of any matter the publication or broad-

casting of which is prohibited by law, or of any matter which is not of public concern and the publication or broadcasting of which is not for the public benefit.

(4) Nothing in this section shall be construed as limiting or abridging any privilege subsisting (otherwise than by virtue of section 4 of the Law of Libel Amendment Act, 1888) immediately before the commencement of this Act.

25.—An agreement for indemnifying any person against civil liability for libel in respect of the publication of any matter shall not be unlawful unless at the time of the publication that person knows that the matter is defamatory, and does not reasonably believe there is a good defence to any action brought upon it.

26.—In any action for libel or slander the defendant may give evidence in mitigation of damages that the plaintiff has recovered damages, or has brought actions for damages, for libel or slander in respect of the publication of words to the same effect as the words on which the action is founded, or has received or agreed to receive compensation in respect of any such publication.

27.—(1) The proprietor of every newspaper having a place of business in the State shall, where such proprietor is not a company registered under the Companies Acts, 1908 to 1959, and is not required under the provisions of the Registration of Business Names Act, 1916, to be registered under that Act in respect of the business of carrying on such newspaper, be registered in the manner directed by that Act, and that Act shall apply to such proprietor in like manner as it applies to a firm or individual referred to in section 1 thereof.

(2) Every reference in the Registration of Business Names Act, 1916, to that Act shall be construed as a reference to that Act as extended by subsection (1) of this section.

(3) In this section "newspaper" means any paper containing public news or observations thereon, or consisting wholly or mainly of advertisements, which is printed for sale and is published in the State either periodically or in parts or numbers at intervals not exceeding twenty-six days.

28.—Nothing in this Part shall affect the law relating to criminal libel.

FIRST SCHEDULE
Enactments Repealed

Part I: Acts of the Parliament of Ireland

Session and Chapter	Title
28 Hen. 8, c. 7 (Ir.).	An Act of Slaunder.
2 Geo. 1, c. 20 (Ir.).	An Act to limit the time for Criminal Prosecutions for words spoken.
33 Geo. 3, c. 43 (Ir.).	An Act to remove doubts respecting the functions of juries in cases of libel.

Part II: Acts of the Parliament of the late United Kingdom of Great Britain and Ireland

Session and Chapter	Title
60 Geo. 3 & I Geo. 4, c. 8.	Criminal Libel Act, 1819.
3 & 4 Vic., c. 9.	Parliamentary Papers Act, 1840.
6 & 7 Vic., c. 96.	Libel Act, 1943.
8 & 9 Vic., c. 75.	Libel Act, 1845.
32 & 33 Vic., c. 24.	Newspapers Printers and Reading Rooms Repeal Act, 1869.
44 & 45 Vic., c. 60.	Newspaper Libel and Registration Act, 1881.
51 & 52 Vic., c. 64.	Law of Libel Amendment Act, 1888.
54 & 55 Vic., c. 51.	Slander of Women Act, 1891.

SECOND SCHEDULE
Statements having qualified privilege

Part I: Statements privileged without Explanation or Contradiction

1. A fair and accurate report of any proceedings in public of a house of any legislature (including subordinate or federal legislatures) of any foreign sovereign State or any body which is part of such legislature or any body duly appointed by or under the legislature or executive of such State to hold a public inquiry on a matter of public importance.

2. A fair and accurate report any proceedings in public of an international organization of which the State or the Government is a member or of any international conference to which the Government sends a representative.

3. A fair and accurate report of any proceedings in public of the International Court of Justice and any other judicial or arbitral tribunal deciding matters in dispute between States.

4. A fair and accurate report of any proceedings before a court (including a courtmartial) exercising jurisdiction under the law of any legislature (including subordinate or federal legislatures) of any foreign sovereign State.

5. A fair and accurate copy of or extract from any register kept in pursuance of any law which is open to inspection by the public or of any other document which is required by law to be open to inspection by the public.

6. Any notice or advertisement published by or on the authority of any court in the State or in Northern Ireland or any Judge or officer of such a court

Part II: Statements privileged subject to Explanation or Contradiction

1. A fair and accurate report of the findings or decision of any of the following associations, whether formed in the State or Northern Ireland, or of any committee or governing body thereof, that is to say:

      (*a*) an association for the purpose of promoting or encouraging the exercise of or interest in any art, science, religion or learning, and empowered by its constitution to exercise control over or adjudicate upon matters of interest or concern to the association or the actions or conduct of any persons subject to such control or adjudication;

(*b*) an association for the purpose of promoting or safeguarding the interests of any trade, business, industry or profession or of the persons carrying on or engaged in any trade, business, industry or profession and empowered by its constitution to exercise control over or adjudicate upon matters connected with the trade, business, industry or profession or the actions or conductor those persons;

(*c*) an association for the purpose of promoting or safeguarding the interests of any game, sport or pastime, to the playing or exercise of which members of the public are invited or admitted, and empowered by its constitution to exercise control over or adjudicate upon persons connected with or taking part in the game, sport or pastime;

being a finding or decision relating to a person who is a member of or is subject by virtue of any contract to the control of the association.

2. A fair and accurate report of the proceedings at any public meeting held in the State or Northern Ireland, being a meeting *bona fide* and lawfully held for a lawful purpose and for the furtherance or discussion of any matter of public concern whether the admission to the meeting is general or restricted.

3. A fair and accurate report of the proceedings at any meeting or sitting of—

(*a*) any local authority, or committee of a local authority or local authorities, and any corresponding authority, or committee thereof, in Northern Ireland;

(*b*) any Judge or Justice acting otherwise than as a court exercising judicial authority and any corresponding person so acting in Northern Ireland;

(*c*) any commission, tribunal, committee or person appointed, whether in the State or Northern Ireland, for the purposes of any inquiry under statutory authority;

(*d*) any person appointed by a local authority to hold a local inquiry in pursuance of an Act of the Oireachtas and any person appointed by a corresponding authority in Northern

Ireland to hold a local inquiry in pursuance of statutory
authority;
(*e*) any other tribunal, board, committee or body constituted
by or under, and exercising functions under, statutory
authority, whether in the State or Northern Ireland;
not being a meeting or sitting admission to which is not allowed to
representatives of the press and other members of the public.

4. A fair and accurate report of the proceedings at a general meeting,
whether in the State or Northern Ireland, of any company or
association constituted, registered or certified by or under statutory
authority or incorporated by charter, not being, in the case of a
company in the State, a private company within the meaning of the
Companies Acts, 1908 to 1959, or, in the case of a company in
Northern Ireland, a private company within the meaning of the
statutes relating to companies for the time being in force therein.

5. A copy or fair and accurate report or summary of any notice or
other matter issued for the information of the public by or on behalf
of any Government department, local authority or the Commissioner
of the Garda Síochána or by or on behalf of a corresponding
department, authority or officer in Northern Ireland.

DATA PROTECTION ACT, 1988 (No. 25 of 1988)
(Sections 1–8)

ARRANGEMENT OF SECTIONS
Preliminary
1. Interpretation and application of Act.

Protection of Privacy of Individuals with regards to Personal Data
2. Collection, processing, keeping, use and disclosure of personal
data.
3. Right to establish existence of personal data.
4. Right of access.
5. Restriction of right of access.
6. Right of rectification or erasure.
7. Duty of care owed by data controllers and data processors.
8. Disclosure of personal data in certain cases.

Interpretation and application of Act

1.—(1) In this Act, unless the context otherwise requires—

"appropriate authority" has the meaning assigned to it by the Civil Service Regulation Acts, 1956 and 1958;

"back-up data" means data kept only for the purpose of replacing other data in the event of their being lost, destroyed or damaged;

"civil servant" has the meaning assigned to it by the Civil Service Regulation Acts, 1956 and 1958;

"the Commissioner" has the meaning assigned to it by section 9 of this Act;

"company" has the meaning assigned to it by the Companies Act, 1963;

"the Convention" means the Convention for the Protection of Individuals with regard to Automatic Processing of Personal Data done at Strasbourg on the 28th day of January, 1981, the text of which is set out in the First Schedule to this Act.

"the Court" means the Circuit Court;

"data" means information in a form in which it can be processed;

"data controller" means a person who. either alone or with others, controls the contents and use of personal data;

"data equipment" means equipment for processing data;

"data material" means any document or other material used in connection with, or produced by, data equipment;

"data processor" means a person who processes personal data on behalf of a data controller but does not include an employee of a data controller who processes such data in the course of his employment;

"data subject" means an individual who is the subject of personal data;

"direct marketing" includes direct mailing;

"disclosure", in relation to personal data, includes the disclosure of information extracted from such data and the transfer of such data but does not include a disclosure made directly or indirectly by a data controller or a data processor to an employee or agent of his for the purpose of enabling the employee or agent to carry out his duties; and, where the identification of a data subject depends partly on the data and partly on other information in the possession of the data controller, the data shall not be regarded as disclosed unless the other information is also disclosed;

"enforcement notice" means a notice under section 10 of this Act.

"financial institution" means—

> (*a*) a person who holds or has held a licence under section 9 of the Central Bank Act, 1971, or

> (*b*) a person referred to in section 7(4) of that Act;

"information notice" means a notice under section 12 of this Act;

"local authority" means a local authority for the purposes of the Local Government Act, 1941;

"the Minister" means the Minister for Justice;

"personal data" means data relating to a living individual who can be identified either from the data or from the data in conjunction with other information in the possession of the data controller;

"prescribed", in the case of fees, means prescribed by regulations made by the Minister with the consent of the Minister for Finance and, in any other case, means prescribed by regulations made by the Commissioner with the consent of the Minister;

"processing" means performing automatically logical or arithmetical operations on data and includes—

> (*a*) extracting any information constituting the data; and

> (*b*) in relation to a data processor, the use by a data controller of data equipment in the possession of the data processor and any other services provided by him for a data controller;

but does not include an operation performed solely for the purpose of preparing the text of documents;

"prohibition notice" means a notice under section 11 of this Act;

"the register" means the register established and maintained under section 16 of this Act;

and any cognate words shall be construed accordingly.

(2) For the purposes of this Act, data are inaccurate if they are incorrect or misleading as to any matter of fact.

(3) (*a*) An appropriate authority, being a data controller or a data processor, may, as respects all or part of the personal data kept by the authority, designate a civil servant in relation

to whom it is the appropriate authority to be a data controller or a data processor and, while the designation is in force—

(i) the civil servant so designated shall be deemed, for the purposes of this Act, to be a data controller or, as the case may be, a data processor, and

(ii) this Act shall not apply to the authority,

as respects the data concerned.

(*b*) Without prejudice to paragraph (a) of this subsection, the Minister for Defence may, as respects all or part of the personal data kept by him in relation to the Defence Forces, designate an officer of the Permanent Defence Force who holds a commissioned rank therein to be data controller or a data processor and, while the designation is in force—

(i) the officer so designated shall be deemed, for the purposes of this Act, to be a data controller or, as the case may be, a data processor, and

(ii) this Act shall not apply to the Minister for Defence,

as respects the data concerned.

(*c*) For the purposes of this Act, as respects any personal data—

(i) where a designation by the relevant appropriate authority under paragraph (a) of this subsection is not in force, a civil servant in relation to whom that authority is the appropriate authority shall be deemed to be its employee and, where such a designation is in force, such a civil servant (other than the civil servant the subject of the designation) shall be deemed to be an employee of the last mentioned civil servant,

(ii) where a designation under paragraph (b) of this subsection is not in force, a member of the Defence Forces shall be deemed to be an employee of the Minister for Defence and, where such a designation is in force, such a member (other than the officer the subject of the designation) shall be deemed to be an employee of that officer, and

(iii) a member of the Garda Síochána (other than the Commissioner of the Garda Síochána) shall be deemed to be an employee of the said Commissioner.

(4) This Act does not apply to—
- (*a*) personal data that in the opinion of the Minister or the Minister for Defence are, or at any time were, kept for the purpose of safeguarding the security of the State;
- (*b*) personal data consisting of information that the person keeping the data is required by law to make available to the public; or
- (*c*) personal data kept by an individual and concerned only with the management of his personal, family or household affairs or kept by an individual only for recreational purposes.

Collection, processing, keeping, use and disclosure of personal data

2.—(1) A data controller shall, as respects personal data kept by him, comply with the following provisions:
- (*a*) the data or, as the case may be, the information constituting the data shall have been obtained, and the data shall be processed, fairly,
- (*b*) the data shall be accurate and, where necessary, kept up to date,
- (*c*) the data—
  - (i)   shall be kept only for one or more specified and lawful purposes,
  - (ii) shall not be used or disclosed in any manner incompatible with that purpose or those purposes,
  - (iii) shall be adequate, relevant and not excessive in relation to that purpose or those purposes, and
  - (iv) shall not be kept for longer than is necessary for that purpose or those purposes,
- (*d*) appropriate security measures shall be taken against unauthorised access to, or alteration, disclosure or destruction of, the data and against their accidental loss or destruction.

(2) A data processor shall, as respects personal data processed by him, comply with paragraph (d) of subsection (1) of this section.

(3) Paragraph(a) of the said subsection (1) does not apply to information intended for inclusion in data, or to data, kept for a purpose mentioned in section 5(1)(a) of this Act, in any case in which the application of that paragraph to the data would be likely

to prejudice any of the matters mentioned in the said section 5(1)(a).

(4) Paragraph (b) of the said subsection (1) does not apply to back-up data.

(5)(*a*) Paragraph (c)(iv) of the said subsection (1) does not apply to personal data kept for historical, statistical or research purposes, and

    (*b*) the data or, as the case may be, the information constituting such data shall not be regarded for the purposes of paragraph (a) of the said subsection as having been obtained unfairly by reason only that its use for any such purpose was not disclosed when it was obtained,

if the data are not used in such a way that damage or distress is, or is likely to be, caused to any data subject.

(6)(*a*) The Minister may, for the purpose of providing additional safeguards in relation to personal data as to racial origin, political opinions, religious or other beliefs, physical or mental health, sexual life or criminal convictions, by regulations amend subsection (1) of this section,

    (*b*) Regulations under this section may make different provision in relation to data of different descriptions.

    (*c*) References in this Act to subsection (1) of this section or to a provision of that subsection shall be construed in accordance with any amendment under this section.

    (*d*) Regulations under this section shall be made only after consultation with any other Minister of the Government who, having regard to his functions, ought, in the opinion of the Minister, to be consulted.

    (*e*) Where it is proposed to make regulations under this section, a draft of the regulations shall be laid before each House of the Oireachtas and the regulations shall not be made until a resolution approving of the draft shall have been passed by each such House.

(7) Where—

    (*a*) personal data are kept for the purpose of direct marketing, and

    (*b*) the data subject concerned requests the data controller in writing to cease using the data for that purpose,

the data controller shall, as soon as may be and in any event not more than 40 days after the request has been given or sent to him—

   (i) if the data are kept only for the purpose aforesaid,
        erase the data,

  (ii) if the data are kept for that purpose and other purposes,
        cease using the data for that purpose, and

 (iii) notify the data subject in writing accordingly and,
        where appropriate, inform him of those other purposes.

Right to establish existence of personal data

3.—An individual who believes that a person keeps personal data
shall, if he so requests the person in writing—

   (*a*) be informed by the person whether he keeps any such
          data, and

   (*b*) if he does; be given by the person a description of the
          data and the purposes for which they are kept,

as soon as may be and in any event not more than 21 days
after the request has been given or sent to him.

Right of access

4.—(1)(*a*) Subject to the provisions of this Act, an individual
           shall, if he so requests a data controller in writing—

      (i) be informed by the data controller whether the data
           kept by him include personal data relating to the
           individual, and

     (ii) be supplied by the data controller with a copy of the
           information constituting any such data, as soon as
           may be and in any event not more than 40 days after
           compliance by the individual with the provisions of
           this section; and, where any of the information is
           expressed in terms that are not intelligible to the
           average person without explanation, the information
           shall be accompanied by an explanation of those terms.

   (*b*) A request for the information specified in sub-paragraph
          (i) of subsection (1)(a) of this section shall, in the absence
          of any indication to the contrary, be treated as including
          a request for a copy of the information specified in
          sub-paragraph (ii) of the said subsection (1)(a).

   (*c*) (i)   A fee may be payable to the data controller concerned
              in respect of such a request as aforesaid and the

           amount thereof shall not exceed such amount as may be prescribed or an amount that in the opinion of the Commissioner is reasonable, having regard to the estimated cost to the data controller of compliance with the request, whichever is the lesser.

  (ii) A fee paid by an individual to a data controller under sub-paragraph (i) of this paragraph shall be returned to him if his request is not complied with or the data controller rectifies or supplements, or erases part of, the data concerned (and thereby materially modifies the data) or erases all of the data on the application of the individual or in accordance with an enforcement notice or an order of a court.

(2) Where pursuant to provision made in that behalf under this Act there are separate entries in the register in respect of data kept by a data controller for different purposes, subsection (1) of this section shall apply as if it provided for the making of a separate request and the payment of a separate fee in respect of the data to which each entry relates.

(3) An individual making a request under this section shall supply the data controller concerned with such information as he may reasonably require in order to satisfy himself of the identity of the individual and to locate any relevant personal data or information.

(4) Nothing in subsection (1) of this section obliges a data controller to disclose to a data subject personal data relating to another individual unless that other individual has consented to the disclosure:

Provided that, where the circumstances are such that it would be reasonable for the data controller to conclude that, if any particulars identifying that other individual were omitted, the data could then be disclosed as aforesaid without his being thereby identified to the data subject, the data controller shall be obliged to disclose the data to the data subject with the omission of those particulars.

(5) Information supplied pursuant to a request under subsection (1) of this section may take account of any amendment of the personal data concerned made since the receipt of the request by the data controller (being an amendment that would have been made irrespective of the receipt of the request) but not of any other amendment.

(6) (*a*) A request by an individual under subsection (1) of this section in relation to the results of an examination at

which he was a candidate shall be deemed, for the purposes
of this section, to be made on—
  (i) the date of the first publication of the results of the
       examination, or
  (ii) the date of the request,
whichever is the later; and paragraph (a) of the said subsection
(1) shall be construed and have effect in relation to such a
request as if for "40 days" there were substituted "60 days".
  (*b*) In this subsection "examination" means any process for
       determining the knowledge, intelligence, skill or ability of
       a person by reference to his performance in any test, work
       or other activity.
  (7) A notification of a refusal of a request made by an individual
under and in compliance with the preceding provisions of this section
shall be in writing and shall include a statement of the reasons for
the refusal and an indication that the individual may complain to
the Commissioner about the refusal.
  (8) (*a*) If and whenever the Minister considers it desirable in the
          interests of data subjects to do so and by regulations so
          declares, the application of this section to personal data—
          (i) relating to physical or mental health, or
          (ii) kept for, or obtained in the course of, carrying out
               social work by a Minister of the Government, a local
               authority, a health board or a specified voluntary
               organisation or other body,
       may be modified by the regulations in such manner, in such
       circumstances, subject to such safeguards and to such extent
       as may be specified therein.
  (*b*) Regulations under paragraph (a) of this subsection shall
       be made only after consultation with the Minister for
       Health and any other Minister of the Government who,
       having regard to his functions, ought, in the opinion of
       the Minister, to be consulted and may make different
       provision in relation to data of different descriptions.

Restriction of right of access

  5.—(1) Section 4 of this Act does not apply to personal data—
  (*a*) kept for the purpose of preventing, detecting or investi-
       gating offences, apprehending or prosecuting offenders or

assessing or collecting any tax, duty or other moneys owed or payable to the State, a local authority or a health board, in any case in which the application of that section to the data would be likely to prejudice any of the matters aforesaid,

(*b*) to which, by virtue of paragraph (a) of this subsection, the said section 4 does not apply and which are kept for the purpose of discharging a function conferred by or under any enactment and consisting of information obtained for such a purpose from a person who had it in his possession for any of the purposes mentioned in paragraph (a) of this subsection,

(*c*) in any case in which the application of that section would be likely to prejudice the security of, or the maintenance of good order and discipline in—

    (i) a prison,

    (ii) a place of detention provided under section 2 of the Prison Act, 1970,

    (iii) a military prison or detention barrack within the meaning of the Defence Act, 1954, or

    (iv) Saint Patrick's Institution,

(*d*) kept for the purpose of performing such functions conferred by or under any enactment as may be specified by regulations made by the Minister, being functions that, in the opinion of the Minister, are designed to protect members of the public against financial loss occasioned by—

    (i) dishonesty, incompetence or malpractice on the part of persons concerned in the provision of banking, insurance, investment or other financial services or in the management of companies or similar organisations, or

    (ii) the conduct of persons who have at any time been adjudicated bankrupt,

in any case in which the application of that section to the data would be likely to prejudice the proper performance of any of those functions,

(*e*) in respect of which the application of that section would be contrary to the interests of protecting the international relations of the State, consisting of an estimate of, or kept for the purpose of estimating, the amount of the liability of the data controller concerned on foot of a claim for the payment of a sum of money, whether in respect of damages or compensation. in any case in which the application of the section would be likely to prejudice the interests of the data controller in relation to the claim.

(g) in respect of which a claim of privilege could be maintained in proceedings in a court in relation to communications between a client and his professional legal advisers or between those advisers,

(h) kept only for the purpose of preparing statistics or carrying out research if the data are not used or disclosed (other than to a person to whom a disclosure of such data may be made in the circumstances specified in section 8 of this Act) for any other purpose and the resulting statistics or the results of the research are not made available in a form that identifies any of the data subjects, or

(i) that are back-up data.

(2) Regulations under subsections (1)(d) and (3)(b) of this section shall be made only after consultation with any other Minister of the Government who, having regard to his functions, ought, in the opinion of the Minister, to be consulted.

(3) (a) Subject to paragraph (b) of this subsection, section 4 of this Act, as modified by any other provisions thereof, shall apply notwithstanding any provision of or made under any enactment or rule of law that is in force immediately before the passing of this Act and prohibits or restricts the disclosure, or authorises the withholding, of information.

(b) If and whenever the Minister is of opinion that a prohibition, restriction or authorisation referred to in paragraph (a) of this subsection in relation to any information ought to prevail in the interests of the data subjects concerned or any other individuals and by regulations so declares, then, while the regulations are in force. the said *paragraph (a)* shall not apply as respects the provision or rule of law concerned and accordingly, section 4 of this Act, as modified as aforesaid, shall not apply in relation to that information.

Right of rectification or erasure

6.—(1) An individual shall, if he so requests in writing a data controller who keeps personal data relating to him, be entitled to have rectified or, where appropriate, erased any such data in relation to which there has been a contravention by the data controller of section 1(2) of this Act; and the data controller shall comply with the request as soon as may be and in any event not more than 40 days after it has been given or sent to him:

Provided that the data controller shall, as respects data that are inaccurate or not kept up to date, be deemed—

    (*a*) to have complied with the request if he supplements the data with a statement (to the terms of which the individual has assented) relating to the matters dealt with by the data, and

    (*b*) if he supplements the data as aforesaid, not to be in contravention of paragraph (b) of the said section 2(1).

(2) On compliance by a data controller with a request under subsection (d) of this subsection, he shall as soon as may be and in any event not more than 40 days after the request has been or sent to him, notify—

    (*a*) the individual making the request, and

    (*b*) if such compliance materially modifies the data concerned, any person to whom the data were disclosed during the period of 12 months immediately before the giving or sending of the request,

of the rectification, erasure or statement concerned.

Duty of care owed by data controllers and data processors

7.—For the purposes of the law of torts and to the extent that that law does not so provide, a person, being a data controller or a data processor, shall, so far as regards the collection by him of personal data or information intended for inclusion in such data or his dealing with such data, owe a duty of care to the data subject concerned:

Provided that, for the purposes only of this section, a data controller shall be deemed to have complied with the provisions of section 2(1)(b) of this Act if and so long as the personal data concerned accurately record data or other information received or obtained by him from the data subject or a third party and include (and, if the data are disclosed, the disclosure is accompanied by)—

- (*a*) an indication that the information constituting the data was received or obtained as aforesaid,
- (*b*) if appropriate, an indication that the data subject has informed the data controller that he regards the information as inaccurate or not kept up to date, and
- (*c*) any statement with which, pursuant to this Act, the data are supplemented.

Disclosure of personal data in certain cases

8.—Any restrictions in this Act on the disclosure of personal data do not apply if the disclosure is—

- (*a*) in the opinion of a member of the Garda Síochána not below the rank of chief superintendent or an officer of the Permanent Defence Force who holds an army rank not below that of colonel and is designated by the Minister for Defence under this paragraph, required for the purpose of safeguarding the security of the State,
- (*b*) required for the purpose of preventing, detecting or investigating offences, apprehending or prosecuting offenders or assessing or collecting any tax, duty or other moneys owed or payable to the State, a local authority or a health board, in any case in which the application of those restrictions would be likely to prejudice any of the matters aforesaid,
- (*c*) required in the interests of protecting the international relations of the State,
- (*d*) required urgently to prevent injury or other damage to the health of a person or serious loss of or damage to property,
- (*e*) required by or under any enactment or by a rule of law or order of a court,
- (*f*) required for the purposes of obtaining legal advice or for the purposes of, or in the course of, legal proceedings in which the person making the disclosure is a party or a witness,
- (*g*) made to the data subject concerned or to a person acting on his behalf, or
- (*h*) made at the request or with the consent of the data subject or a person acting on his behalf.

APPENDIX 3

National Union of Journalists Code of Conduct

1. A journalist has a duty to maintain the highest professional and ethical standards.

2. A journalist shall at all times defend the principle of the freedom of the Press and other media in reiaflon to the collection of information and the expression of comment and criticism. He/she shall strive to eliminate distortion, news suppression and censorship.

3. A journalist shall strive to ensure that the information he/she disseminates is fair and accurate, avoid the expression of comment and conjecture as established fact and falsification by distortion, selection or misrepresentation.

4. A journalist shall rectify promptly any harmful inaccuracies, ensure that correction and apologies receive due prominence and afford the right of reply to persons criticised when the issue is of sufficient importance.

5. A journalist shall obtain information, photographs and illustrations only by. straightforward means. The use of other means can be justified only by over-riding considerations of the public interest. The journlist is entitled to exercise a personal conscientious objection to the use of such means.

6. Subject to the justification by over-riding considerations of the public interest, a journalist shall do nothing which entails intrusion into private grief and distress.

7. A journalist shall protect confidential sources of information.

8. A journalist shall not accept bribes nor shall he/she allow other inducements to influence the performance of his/her professional duties.

9. A journalist shall not lend himself/herself to the distortion or suppression of the truth because of advertising or other considerations.

10. A journalist shall only mention a person's race, colour, creed, illegitimacy, marital status (or lack of it), gender or sexual orientation if this information is strictly relevant. A journalist shall neither originate nor process material which encourages discrimination on any of the above-mentioned grounds.

11. A journalist shall not take private advantage of information gained in the course of his/her duties, before the information is public knowledge.

12. A journalist shall not by way of statement, voice or appearance endorse by advertisement any commercial product or service save for the promotion of his/her own work or of the medium by which he/she is employed.